I0797295

ENDORSEMENTS

Before you dive into *Infinite Edge*, I wanted you to hear from some of the extraordinary people I've had the privilege to learn from, work with and be challenged by. These leaders have shaped my journey, and now they're part of yours too. What follows are short messages from some close friends and mentors, all of whom are world-class performers – each offering their insight into this book, this system and the Edge you're about to build.

"This book captures what it truly takes to win with humility, discipline and purpose."

Kevin Sinfield, CBE, England national rugby coach

"Infinite Edge *is about more than performance – it's about building the mental strength and authenticity to achieve at the highest level, in sport, business and life."*

Dame Kelly Holmes, double Olympic gold medallist

"James Vincent has spent decades studying what separates the great from the truly elite – and this book is the result. He distils the mental framework behind the world's most consistent winners into a system that's clear, coachable and built to last. If you want to win once, chase a goal. But if you want to keep winning, you need an inner edge. This book shows you how to build it."

Dr. Marshall Goldsmith, *New York Times* bestselling author of *What Got You Here Won't Get You There*

*"*Infinite Edge *is a brilliant blueprint for self-leadership. The daily discipline, clarity and focus needed to build a business with purpose that lasts. If you want to develop the mindset needed to grow a business and win, this is the book to keep by your side."*

Jamie Waller, entrepreneur and author of *The Dyslexic Edge*

"As someone who has spent decades helping business leaders and entrepreneurs reconnect with their purpose, I found Infinite Edge *to be more than a performance manual. It's a call to remember who we truly are and who we can become. James Vincent distils a lifetime of elite coaching into six profound Inner Forces that speak directly to the soul of a Serial Winner. His chapter on the Inner Flame, especially, lit something in me, a beautiful reminder that we don't burn out from weakness, but from disconnection from our values and purpose. This book is timely – we are at a crossroads in business, when technology is meeting the human, providing more challenges and more opportunities. Being in charge of yourself, knowing yourself and being driven by the human inside you will set you apart from the AI victims."*

Penny Power, OBE, business author, speaker and founder of BIP100

"James Vincent is a leader in the coaching space, the Coaches' Coach. His strategies, ideas and insights will take you beyond your next level. Don't just read this book ... study it, implement it and bank it."

Jeffrey Gitomer, author of *The Little Red Book of Selling*

"Your mind is the most powerful force in the universe. James gives you the keys to unleash it."

Uri Geller
www.urigeller.com

"Infinite Edge *brings engineering principles into the arena of performance, showing you how to succeed without sacrificing your happiness or your peace."*

Mo Gawdat, bestselling author and
founder of One Billion Happy

"As you know, there are a million books out there about "mindset." Most are either overcomplicated or – worse – all fluff and no framework. But what James Vincent has created here is different. Infinite Edge *is a full-blown operating system, packed with powerful, practical frameworks designed to help you live and perform at your highest level. What I loved most, though, is that it's not about hacks or hype. It's about identity – becoming someone who doesn't just succeed once, but knows how to do it again and again, under pressure, with clarity and without losing themselves in the process. That's why James's system works. He gives you six Inner Forces that drive lasting performance – and shows you how to build each one like a skill. Confidence. Grit. Focus. Discipline. For leaders, coaches and high performers who are done with surface-level personal development, this is the real work. And not only is it worth reading, more than anything, it's worth doing."*

Marcus Sheridan, bestselling
author of *They Ask You Answer*

"Infinite Edge *is a playbook for becoming the kind of leader people want to follow. James Vincent shows you how to think clearly, lead confidently and win consistently in business and life."*

Daniel Priestley, bestselling author

"James Vincent has created a system that turns mindset into measurable performance. Infinite Edge is a powerful guide for anyone who wants to think and achieve at the highest level.

Jamil Qureshi, world-recognised speaker on all aspects of the psychology of performance

"Infinite Edge *is a performance system with moral compass, drive and purpose at its heart – just what society needs."*

Mary Portas OBE, retail consultant and broadcaster

"James has the rare gift of making big ideas simple and powerful. Infinite Edge *is packed with tools to help you shine in business and in life."*

Stephen Mulhern, television presenter, magician and author

INFINITE
EDGE

INFINITE EDGE

James Vincent

WATKINS

Infinite Edge
James Vincent

This edition first published in the UK and USA in 2026 by
Watkins, an imprint of Watkins Media Limited
Unit 11, Shepperton House
89–93 Shepperton Road
London
N1 3DF

enquiries@watkinspublishing.com

10 9 8 7 6 5 4 3 2 1

Designed by Watkins Publishing
Typeset by Lapiz

Printed and bound in the United Kingdom

The manufacturer's authorised representative in the EU for product safety is:
eucomply OÜ - Pärnu mnt 139b-14, 11317 Tallinn, Estonia,
hello@eucompliancepartner.com, www.eucompliancepartner.com

A CIP record for this book is available from the British Library

ISBN: 978-1-83681-056-8 (Hardback)
ISBN: 978-1-83681-057-5 (eBook)

www.watkinspublishing.com

Note: Some names and identifying details have been changed to protect privacy.
All stories are told with accuracy of experience, but certain individuals are anonymized.

Dedicated to those who aspire to greatness,
who believe there's more in them,
and are willing to train for it.
This is your Edge.

CONTENTS

FOREWORD

BY BRAD SUGARS – THE WORLD #1 BUSINESS COACH

When you've spent decades building a global movement in coaching, you learn to recognize the rare individuals who elevate the work to another level. James Vincent is one of those rare few.

As the world's #1 business coach, I've met and worked alongside some of the finest coaches on the planet. But James stands apart. He is the best I've seen at bringing performance psychology into the world of business and personal achievement. He has made this his life's work, dedicating himself fully to coaching, not just as a profession, but as a purpose.

What makes James exceptional isn't just his knowledge or experience – though those are world class. It's the way he lives what he teaches. He is a man who leads with integrity, balances his devotion to his clients with devotion to his family, and shows up consistently as a great dad, a great husband, a great friend. Coaching, at its core, is about helping people become the best version of themselves. James embodies that truth every single day.

This book, *Infinite Edge*, is the essence of James's life's work. It is practical, it is psychological and it is deeply personal. It provides a pathway to the very highest levels of performance ... not only in business, but in life. Whether you are an entrepreneur, a leader or simply someone determined to get more from yourself, these pages will equip you with the systems, strategies and mindset required to achieve and sustain excellence.

The reason I connect so strongly with James's message is because it reflects the heart of what we believe at ActionCOACH. Our ABoS manifesto reminds us: this is bigger than business. Behind every system installed is a life transformed. A parent present at the dinner table.

A business owner finally sleeping peacefully. A team growing in confidence. Coaching is not just about profits, it's about people. It's not only about scaling companies, it's about strengthening communities. James has always understood this truth at the deepest level, and it comes alive in every chapter of this book.

I am proud to say James and I are brothers in action – men living our legacies side by side. My legacy has been building ActionCOACH, ABoS, and the vision of creating world abundance through business re-education. James's legacy is in helping people think clearer, feel stronger and perform at their absolute best. And here's what makes it even more powerful: we are doing it together, inside ActionCOACH, putting this work into practice globally. We are currently operating in 86 countries, and growing. From boardrooms in London to coffee shops in Florida, from family businesses in Johannesburg to fast-growth enterprises in Tokyo – the message is spreading, the systems are being installed, and lives are being transformed. Every day, we witness not just businesses scaling, but families reconnecting, leaders finding clarity, and communities thriving.

That's why this book matters so much. *Infinite Edge* gives you the tools to step out of chaos and into clarity, to lead yourself and others with confidence, and to build a life and business that truly works. Read it with focus. Reflect on it deeply. And most importantly, act on it with consistency.

Because when you do, you'll see what I see in James Vincent: one of the finest coaches in the world, a man who is living his legacy and a leader who will help you live yours too.

This is not just a book. This is a movement.

Brad Sugars, Founder & Chairman of ActionCOACH
World #1 Business Coach

FOREWORD

BY FRANK DICK, OBE

A winning culture is founded on a learning culture. So, as leaders or coaches, we create a learning environment for those whose lives we have an opportunity to influence.

Books can be things you read, then keep in your bookcase. But they can also be resources that you keep turning to. The best are a learning environment in themselves. *Infinite Edge* is one of the best.

James has brilliantly created a learning environment born of the experience and expertise gained from his deep and successful dive into high-performance coaching in sport, business, the professions and life.

He breaks the mould by creating effective, winning coaching systems and in guiding us in what it takes to lead them.

More than this, he is a game-changer in his clarity of purpose and method in coaching and developing people in this rapidly changing world. He does this by listening to those whose lives he touches, and by understanding their needs, whether professional or personal.

A winning mindset is often proposed in high-performance literature, but is very seldom explored with such understanding and authority as in these pages. James goes beyond ways of thinking to investigating our behaviour, decision-making and indeed how we live our lives. He is acutely aware that being focused on the task at hand should not mean being blinkered to those changes around us that will impact our journey. Whatever our arena, James creates a learning environment that teaches how to become a consistent achiever, and shows us not only how to do things better and differently, but also how to *be* better and different.

So, *Infinite Edge* will help you set your course and advance in the arenas you face now, and will also prepare you for the challenges that are to come. It is more than a rudder and compass; it is a thoughtfully and expertly designed route map.

It's my huge privilege to have written this foreword.

Frank Dick OBE – world-renowned high-performance coach & author

INTRODUCTION

WHERE YOUR EDGE BEGINS

Every era has its champions. Every generation has its leaders. But one thing unites them all: they mastered *themselves* before they mastered anything else.

The world has changed. The tools have evolved. The challenges have shifted. But the principles that drive success – the kind that lasts – have stood the test of time:

- Mental clarity, speed and strength to unleash the power of your mind
- Self-belief and confidence to build yourself from the inside
- Drive, vision and desire to want more and become more
- Discipline and willingness to do what it takes
- Personal growth to become what you're capable of
- Calmness and consistency under pressure to perform when it matters

These aren't passing trends. They're timeless truths, handed down through centuries. Carried by those who dared to be more.

This book is built on those principles. This is the playbook of winners. Used yesterday. Proven today. Built for tomorrow.

Inside these pages, you'll find more than ideas. You'll find strategies – forged through history, tested in business and refined in the minds of the most disciplined, confident and consistent leaders of today – that you can use to fulfil your own goals. To find your own Edge.

Join the greatest minds in history

The idea of Infinite Edge isn't new. It's eternal. The greatest minds in history had one key thing in common: they knew that winning is not a mystery – it's a **mindset**. These principles of success outlast trends and transcend culture and technology:

> *"Knowing others is intelligence; knowing yourself is true wisdom."*
> – Lao Tzu

> *"Opportunities multiply as they are seized."*
> – Sun Tzu

> *"What you think, you become. What you feel, you attract. What you imagine, you create."*
> – The Buddha

> *"We are what we repeatedly do. Excellence, then, is not an act, but a habit."*
> – Aristotle

> *"It's not what happens to you, but how you react to it that matters."*
> – Epictetus

> *"Genius is one percent inspiration and ninety-nine percent perspiration."*
> – Thomas Edison

> *"Act enthusiastic and you'll be enthusiastic."*
> – Dale Carnegie

> *"Most people overestimate what they can do in one year and underestimate what they can do in ten."*
> – Bill Gates

> *"People don't buy what you do. They buy why you do it."*
> – Simon Sinek

These words aren't just echoes from history – they reveal evergreen principles. Truths that have stood firm across empires, eras and evolution. This mindset guided philosophers, built nations and fuelled revolutions of mind and spirit.

And now, I use this shared wisdom to form the foundation of this book – a book built on principles that have always worked … and always will.

Your Edge is waiting

The goal of this book is simple:

> *To help you build a stronger mind, attract bigger opportunities and become the kind of person who doesn't just succeed once – but succeeds for life.*

It's about sharpening your Edge – so that winning becomes *who you are.*

Everyone wants to succeed. But want alone doesn't move the needle. Hope won't build your future. Trying isn't the same as becoming. Lasting success belongs to those who are prepared – those who do the work and build themselves from the inside out.

Think now of the people you admire. I have coached entrepreneurs in many industries; leaders of huge organizations; creatives who want to make a difference; visionaries who want to achieve something great; parents wanting more for their families and themselves; athletes in many sports at grassroots level and Olympic level … People who are making change happen, and building success. In this book we will look at what every successful person has in common. The Edge. Whatever drove you to pick up this book, whatever field you are in, the ideas within can work for *your* goals and *your* objectives.

What creates real change isn't more noise. It's structure. It's system. A way to turn potential into performance – again and again. That's what this book delivers.

Your inner coach

While a great performance coach can guide you, the one who must lead you is already within. You've heard that inner voice before – the one that challenges your excuses, nudges you forward and dares you to become more? That voice is your inner coach. This book will help you sharpen that voice. Strengthen it. And turn it into your most powerful advantage. And that advantage is Infinite.

The boldest version of you isn't something to wait for – it's something you choose. And when you act like this is your time … it starts to become true.

Here's what you'll build, by reading this book:

- **Mind Power** – mental clarity, speed, strength and control
- **Confidence** – built from the inside out, one belief and one action at a time
- **Inner Flame** – a desire that fuels purpose-driven action
- **Persistence** – the identity of someone who keeps going, no matter what
- **Performance Edge** – mastery over your skills, with execution
- **Ice-cool Composure** – challenge becomes a place where you thrive.

Put it all together – and you won't just win once. You'll become the kind of person who wins for life. That's your Infinite Edge.

So, the question isn't: *Is it possible?*
The question is: *What will you do with it?*

YOUR MIND IS YOUR EDGE

You can build your mind just like you build a muscle, and train it like an athlete:

- You can practise resilience
- You can train sharper thinking
- You can develop stronger beliefs
- You don't need "more time" – you need more depth.

… But only if you're willing to move past the illusion of ease and into the practice of mastery.

Why I wrote this book – and why it works

I didn't learn these lessons from books alone. I lived them.

I grew up in the Yorkshire countryside – where grit wasn't taught, it was lived. Through sport, I learned discipline, ambition, and how to push through challenges. I went on to represent my country at the highest level and, later, to coach Olympians and elite business leaders around the world.

For over 50,000 hours, I've been obsessed with one question: What makes people truly unstoppable? I've studied this question, tested it, and coached it in life, sport and business.

I've faced setbacks and used them as fuel. I've lived with dyslexia and ADHD – and turned them into strengths. Those strengths weren't random. They were built – shaped by purpose and sharpened through persistence.

Purpose changed everything. Coaching became my calling. And through it, I discovered a simple truth:

Potential isn't something you're born with. It's something you build.

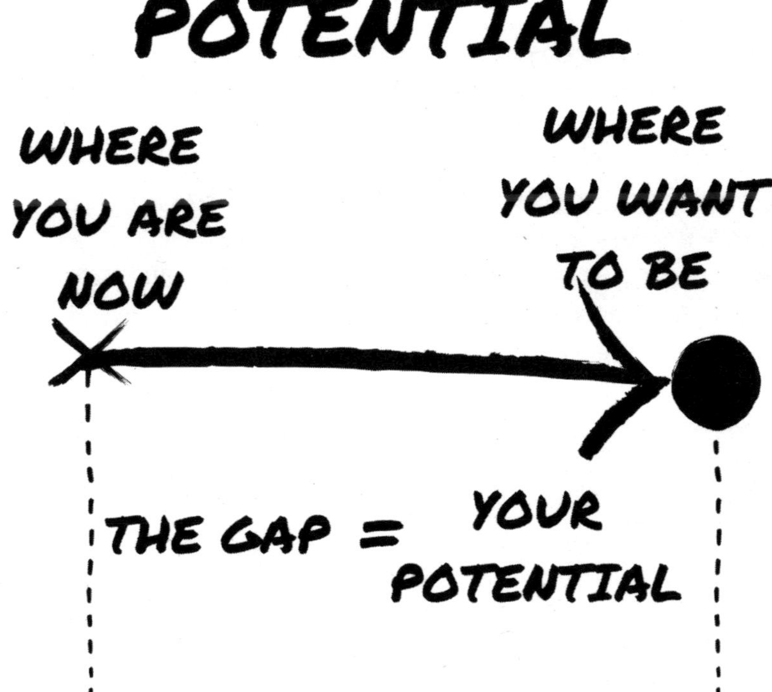

Potential lives in the gap between where you are ... and where you could be. The real question isn't whether it exists. It's whether you're willing to *close that gap*.

This book is your blueprint. Not just to win once – but to build a life where success becomes who you are.

TWO QUESTIONS BEFORE YOU BEGIN

Before you turn the next page, pause and answer these two questions. Be honest. Be bold.

These two questions are your invitation to step into a bigger version of yourself. Because the boldest version of you? It's already inside you – waiting for permission to lead.

Q1: What bold move are you resisting, because of fear, doubt or judgement?
Say it. Name it. That's how you take back power.

Q2: If success was guaranteed, how far would you go?
Write your real answer. The one that scares and excites you in equal measure. How big do you dare to dream?

Your answers are a challenge. You are the greatest project of your life. And the time to start building what you want is now.

Because if you don't apply what's already inside you, you'll never discover just how far you could go. And few regrets are heavier than knowing you could have been more ... if only you'd acted.

"The hardest truth to face isn't failure – it's meeting the version of yourself you never became."

James Vincent

How to use this book

Success doesn't arrive by accident. It's always *earned.*

This isn't a book to sit quietly on a shelf. *Infinite Edge* is to be studied, lived and revisited – like a coach who accompanies you through your day. Because success doesn't come from reading alone – it comes from what you *do* with what you read. And the more you engage with it, the more it will give back.

As you read this book, there will be moments that catch you off guard – insights that feel like they were written just for you. Pay attention to those. That's your Edge speaking.

When you begin to apply the principles in *Infinite Edge* – day by day, habit by habit – you'll feel it. Progress will speed up. Decisions will get easier. And success will start chasing you – for what you're doing and, most importantly, for who you're becoming.

A system is only as strong as your ability to use it. That's why in every chapter, you'll find practical tools that bring the principles to life. These tools will help you apply the ideas in real time. Because insight without action is wasted potential. Use them. Print them out. Live with them. Let them become part of your system. That's how winning becomes who you are.

Here's how to get the most from reading this book:

1. **Begin with desire**. Your hunger to grow is your greatest asset. So, ask yourself now:

   Why does this matter to me?
   What am I building?
   Who am I becoming?

   Let your answers pull you forward.

2. **Pause to reflect**. Don't rush. Read a chapter at a time. Stop often. Ask yourself:

   How does this apply to me?
   Where can I use this today?

That's where the magic is – not in the words, but in what you do with them.

3. **Keep a pen and journal nearby**. Mark the pages that speak to you. Use symbols – a star, a tick, a box, a heart – when something resonates. Jot down your thoughts. Use this as your personal playbook.

4. **Apply something after every chapter**. Pick one idea per chapter. Action it immediately. Knowledge isn't power. *Applied* knowledge is. That's how transformation begins – one small move at a time.

5. **Read your notes monthly**. Remind yourself of what matters. Let repetition turn insight into instinct.

6. **Re-read the book every year**. This isn't a one-time read. It will grow with you. Each year, you'll be different. And this book will meet you there.

7. **Pair the book with the audiobook**. Want it to land even deeper? Listen while you read. Eyes on the page. Ears on the message. Double the input. Deeper the impact.

8. **Share with others**. Think about what stood out to you. Teach it to someone else. When you teach, you don't just remember – you *own* it. If this book helps you – pass it on. Write a note inside the front cover: *"This book improved my life. I thought of you. I know it can do the same for you."*

Meet the six Inner Forces

We are now going to look at the principles that build your Infinite Edge. The six Inner Forces that can shape how you think, act, perform and lead.

This is a preview, not a pressure. A spark, not a sprint. You don't need to grasp everything yet. Each chapter will explain in more detail, step by step as the book unfolds, with coaching insights and practical tools to help you apply them in your world.

Force 1. Mind Power: your mental foundation

We will explore how your subconscious is your soil – it grows whatever you plant. Fear or belief. Doubt or direction. Your mind grows what it's fed. You can install new thought patterns, override limits and train belief like a skill.

We will also look at flow, which is where preparation meets stretch – and effort disappears.

Force 2. Confidence LOOP: where belief becomes identity

Confidence is a force, and you build it. You don't wait for it. You harness it, deliberately and repeatedly. Confidence can start with a whisper, not a roar. The softest "Maybe I can ..." is where your Edge begins.

You don't need to kill doubt – just stop feeding it. Letting go creates space. And space is where belief can breathe. And self-belief breeds courage.

Force 3. Inner Flame: where motivation ignites

Motivation is your "motive for action".

Your flame burns brightest when your purpose, values, responsibility and impact align. It's the internal fire that says, "This matters – and I will act."

This chapter is your invitation to live an inspired life. Inspiration is "purpose on fire" – and it fuels infinite action.

Force 4. Refuse to Lose: what sets you apart

Motivation and desire start the fire, but persistence keeps it burning. Most people want to win, but only the relentless Refuse to Lose. Persistence is your Edge in motion, your mental wiring that says, "I go again."

Your beliefs about persistence shape your ability to win. Because in your hardest moment, logic won't carry you – your beliefs and persistence will. That's how you keep going when most quit.

Force 5. Performance Edge: skill and focus

The most powerful and successful people aren't always the most gifted – they're the most focused. The elite aren't born super-human – they choose mastery, then let time, repetition and consistency do its work.

Skill is trainable. Mastery is a choice. A lifestyle. You don't need to be gifted – you need to be *deliberate*.

READ. ACT. BECOME.

Every page, every prompt, every principle in this book is here for one reason: To move you forward.

Not just in what you *do* – but in *who you become* and how you show up to make the world better.

Own your Infinite Edge ... because no motivation is greater than who you will become in the process.

That's the deeper truth of growth. Not the job title. Not the trophy, money or applause. The *real* reward is the person you become on the journey:

- Your mindset will sharpen
- Your discipline will deepen
- Your confidence will grow.

And little by little – your identity will evolve.

So read this book. Study it. Share it. And most of all – *live* it. Because the greatest success story isn't printed on these pages. It's the one you're about to write. And it begins the moment you decide to step fully into the person you're here to be.

Force 6. Ice-cool Composure: power under pressure

Calmness isn't passive – it's power under pressure. In this chapter we look at how to train your nervous system; how to own your internal state and emotional reactions.

Pressure doesn't break you – poor inner leadership does. Composure is more than a moment – it's an identity.

Why this book will change you

Each of the six Inner Forces will be unpacked, explained and brought to life through real stories, clear coaching and practical tools. You're not alone on this journey. I'll guide you through every step. What matters most is that you've started. You've opened the book. From here, everything gets clearer – and your Edge gets sharper.

By mastering the six Inner Forces, you'll equip yourself with the tools to attract success in every area of life – no matter who you are, where you're starting from, or what industry or field you're in. And that's your Infinite Edge.

Success doesn't chase people – it's drawn to those who develop the mindset, habits and consistency to *earn* it.

Apply what's inside this book, and the shift will be undeniable. Because when you do the inner work, the outer results follow. You'll develop:

- **A powerful mind**: You'll stop reacting to life, and start leading it. Your thoughts will work *for* you, not *against* you.
- **Confidence**: The kind that doesn't waver. Grounded belief in yourself, even when the challenge is big and the stakes are high.
- **Desire**: A fire that fuels action. Drive that moves you when others pause. Hunger that doesn't burn out.
- **Persistence**: The ability to keep going, through doubt, failure and fatigue. You'll become someone who finishes what they start.
- **Skill**: Not just talent, but true mastery. The kind that separates high performers from everyone else.
- **Consistency**: Because one win doesn't build a legacy. You'll build the habit of succeeding – again and again. And you'll do it with Ice-cool Composure.

The only thing left to do now is ... start.

Here's to your future. Let's see who you become.

FORCE 1
MIND POWER

"We become what we think about."

Earl Nightingale

Your mind is powerful beyond measure – but only if you understand how it works. The first truth you must accept is this: your mind was not designed to make you happy. Its primary job is to keep you alive. That means it is wired to detect threats, predict problems and cling to the familiar – even if the familiar is what's been holding you back. Until you grasp this design and work with it, you'll forever feel like you're wrestling against yourself.

To unlock your full Mind Power, you must stop fighting it. You must learn to direct it – with clarity, purpose and intention. And that begins with understanding more about how your mind can be your biggest asset.

Your mind is designed to:

Learn and absorb

Your mind is constantly soaking up information – through every book you read, every conversation you have, every success and every mistake. Like tree roots searching for water, your mind seeks out nutrients: knowledge, insight, feedback and lessons.

But when you stop learning – when you stay stuck in old beliefs or avoid new ideas – you starve your mind. And like a malnourished tree, you begin to weaken, slowly and silently.

To grow, you must feed your mind *intentionally*. This is your first duty: absorb the good stuff. And reject the bad.

Change and adapt

Absorbing alone isn't enough. A tree doesn't just take in water – it channels that water into growth. The same is true for your mind. If you learn something new but don't act on it, you've missed the point.

True power lies in your ability to change and adapt. To evolve your thinking, adjust your actions and change direction when life demands it. The most powerful minds aren't the ones that know the most – they're the ones that *adapt the fastest*.

Seek stability

The third purpose of your mind is to seek stability. Just as a tree's roots can anchor it through storms, your mind can anchor you through setbacks, criticism and fear. If your roots are shallow – built on fragile ego or external validation – the smallest gust of wind can knock you over. But if your roots are deep – grounded in purpose and inner strength – no storm can destroy you. A high-performing mind learns quickly and adjusts intelligently, and it *holds strong* – even when life tries to knock it over.

Your subconscious: the silent operator

Behind every thought, decision or feeling lies your subconscious mind. It's the silent operator keeping you alive right now, regulating your heartbeat, breathing and digestion, and also hosting your thoughts, emotions and behaviours.

Your subconscious mind doesn't argue or filter – it simply accepts what it's repeatedly told. Think of your subconscious as the most fertile soil on Earth. Whatever seeds you plant – fear or faith, doubt or belief, anxiety or confidence – it will grow.

Let's borrow the metaphor from *Jack and the Beanstalk*. Jack didn't plant just any seed. He planted a *magic* one. And when he did, it grew sky-high overnight, giving him access to an entirely new world. Your subconscious mind:

- **Is always listening** – especially to repetition, emotion and imagery.
- **Can't tell the difference** between what's vividly imagined and what's real.

- **Controls 95 per cent of your behaviour** – silently running your habits, responses and emotional reactions.
- **Thrives on consistency** – both positive and negative.

So, when you say things like "I always mess up", your subconscious treats that as truth. It installs it like software. But if you feed it with "I am improving every day", it installs *that* truth – and starts adjusting your internal systems to match it.

Here's how that shows up:

- Belief nurtured consistently becomes self-confidence.
- Self-confidence fuels action.
- Action delivers results.

On the flipside:

- Doubt planted over time becomes hesitation.
- Hesitation becomes inaction.
- Inaction becomes regret.

That's the power of the subconscious. Whatever you feed it, it multiplies.

How to program your mind

The subconscious mind is not just a hidden part of you – it's the most powerful force you possess. Understanding this isn't mystical – it's neuroscience. The thoughts you repeat, the images you rehearse, the beliefs you accept without question, all become your habits and default behaviours.

To train your subconscious, you must be intentional with the inputs. There are numerous techniques to do this, and you can start today. We are going to look at:

- **Visualization**: See your success ahead, clearly and repeatedly.
- **Affirmations**: Speak powerful goals, beliefs and truths, with feeling and frequency.
- **Emotion**: Link your desires with strong positive emotions.
- **Repetition**: The brain wires through repetition. Rehearse the reality you want.

"No one can carry your ambition for you. When you take full responsibility, momentum begins – and it's yours to keep."

James Vincent

Don't limit your growth

The mistake most people make? They plant weeds and wonder why their garden won't bloom. They repeat doubts. They visualize failure. They say things like "I always mess up interviews" or "I'm terrible at public speaking", and the subconscious, loyal and obedient, wires that belief into the system.

But if you flip the thinking? If you plant belief, if you water it with repetition and protect it with focus, your subconscious will take it from there:

- It will grow the right thoughts.
- It will steer your actions.
- It will quietly and faithfully create alignment between your inner world, your outer life and your future goals.

LET'S PUT THIS INTO ACTION, RIGHT NOW

And you can start work today. Your first and last thoughts of the day matter – that's when your subconscious is most open. Don't waste that window by doomscrolling or negative thinking. Instead, give your mind clear instructions, like a captain or director briefing their team before a match or performance. Tonight, when you lie in bed, try this:

- Picture what you want.
- Say it with certainty.
- Make it vivid.
- Repeat it out loud.

Repeat the words in the morning, right after waking. Then trust your subconscious mind to do what is does best: grow.

Doing the deep practice

Here's where most people get this wrong: they rush to outcomes. They crave the applause. They focus on wealth. They want mastery without the work of repetition. They chase the fruit before they've fed the roots. But nature doesn't work that way – and neither does greatness.

You see, the top performers in the world don't pursue speed for speed's sake. They pursue Purpose first, and then Precision, Pattern and Practice. They obsess over the deep, invisible work – the kind that compounds beneath the surface. That's what Daniel Coyle calls "deep practice".

So, what is deep practice? It is the art of slowing down, of breaking a skill into parts, of entering that sacred zone just beyond your current limits – where you fail, adjust, repeat and refine. It's deliberate. It's uncomfortable. And it's where growth lives.

- Every time you stop to reflect ...
- Every time you rehearse a line or visualize a move ...
- Every time you sit in the heat of honest feedback ...

... you train your mind and you rewire it.

You fire a new neural pathway, a new circuit. Then fire it again. And with each repetition, your brain lays down insulation – a biological substance called myelin. It wraps around that circuit like tape on a wire. The thicker the myelin, the faster and more accurate your thoughts become.

The best don't think faster because they were born smarter. They think faster because they've built better circuits. This is not magic or luck. This is skill-building, plain and simple.

THE POWER OF DEEP PRACTICE

Clarissa was an ordinary 13-year-old clarinet player. She practised because she was told to.

Then one day something changed. She heard a jazz version of a song called *Golden Wedding*. It moved her. It lit a fire inside. She picked up her clarinet and entered a state of deep practice.

Clarissa played two notes. Stopped. Reflected. Tried again – slower. She corrected herself. She hummed the rhythm. She visualized the movement. She tried once more. And in just six minutes, Clarissa achieved what most students would require a month to accomplish.

Now, ask yourself: what made the difference?

It wasn't talent. It wasn't time. It was *how* she practised.

This young musician didn't go through the motions. She connected a purpose to the jazz and then thought with precision and pattern, and went through a period of focused deep practice. And she came out more skilled on the other side.

Repetition with intention

Let's speak plainly – Tiger Woods was not a miracle. He was a *method*. Yes, the world called him a prodigy. Yes, his swing stunned experts. But if you look closely, you'll see something far more powerful than natural talent – you'll see the result of tiny, deliberate acts, repeated thousands of times – not just by the body, but by his mind.

By the time Tiger could walk, he was watching his father hit balls at the driving range. At age two, he wasn't simply swinging a club – he was building neurological circuits. He was learning to focus, to visualize. To adjust his movements, to control his breath. To feel pressure – and to welcome it.

This was repetition with intention. And that, as Daniel Coyle explains, is the birthplace of skill: "The firing of the circuit is paramount ... Myelin doesn't care who you are – it cares what you do."

And what did Tiger do? He watched. He mimicked. He visualized the perfect shot over and over, years before it counted. He studied the posture of champions. He rehearsed pressure moments in his mind long before he stood on the green at Augusta.

Every swing fired a circuit. Every rehearsal wrapped it in myelin. And with each layer, his mind grew faster, sharper and more automatic.

What looked like genius at 21 was simply the compound interest of focus. It wasn't mystery. It was mastery.

And *that* is your invitation. Whatever the skill you want to improve, you can do it through repetition. You need to fire the circuit. And then fire it again.

The mind, like the body, becomes what you feed it.

If you train it early, often and deeply – you can achieve your goals. Greatness is not reserved for the chosen few. It is built by those who show up – deliberately and daily.

Put your subconscious to work

The same strategy holds true for any goal you have. Would you like more emotional control in high-stakes meetings? Then don't just hope for it. *Rehearse* the pressure. Mentally walk yourself through the tension, the tone, the turning point – until it becomes familiar.

Would you like to make faster, sharper decisions? Then practise slowing them down. Break each one into parts. Observe how you think. Adjust how you respond.

Would you like to radiate confidence with customers? Then train your inner voice. What you say to yourself each morning and evening becomes what others hear from you each day.

These aren't motivational gimmicks. They are mental reps.

And like Tiger's swing or the Williams sisters' footwork, every repetition counts. Because every time you repeat a thought, a behaviour or a reaction, your brain makes a choice: install new ideas or reinforce the old.

And here's the best part: **you are in charge of what gets repeated.** You are not a slave to your moods. You are not stuck with the wiring you were born with. You are the architect of your mind – and repetition is your most powerful tool. So, choose your reps wisely. Feed the right roots. And train your mindset like your greatness depends on it.

Because it does.

How to build your Mind Power

Mind Power isn't wishful thinking – it's neurological. It's built like a muscle. It's planted like a tree. And if you learn to train your brain like the greats do, there is no area of your life that won't benefit from it. Here's how to build your Mind Power, even on your toughest days:

Observe before you act
Slow down, notice what's happening and take the uncomfortable path. For example: Serena Williams reviews every point, asking what she can control before the next serve.

Repeat with purpose
Practise deliberately and reconnect to your vision every time motivation dips. For example: Kobe Bryant shot the same move thousands of times, not for volume, but for precision.

Visualize your future self
See who you are becoming, and act today from that identity. For example: Michael Phelps visualized every race in detail – down to the water splashing in his goggles.

Fail well
Mistakes don't break you, they build you. Each one is a lesson. For example: Lionel Messi missed more than 20 penalties early in his career – each one sharpened him.

Stay in the stretch zone
Growth lives in discomfort. When comfort returns, push again. For example: Usain Bolt hated early-morning training, but he stayed in the grind until speed became second nature.

Mental mastery

Your thoughts are not mere reactions to external stimuli – they are powerful forces that shape your reality. By consciously directing your thoughts, you can influence your emotions, behaviours and, ultimately, your destiny. This is the essence of "mental mastery" – the ability to choose your thoughts and align them with your goals.

Your mind is not a passive observer of your life – it's an active participant, shaping your experiences and outcomes. By understanding its purpose and learning to direct it intentionally, you unlock the door to limitless potential. Embrace the power of your mind, and you will transform your life in ways you never imagined. Every time you:

- Wake up and do the work when no one's watching
- Stay true to your vision while others quit
- Reflect, revise and rebuild when things feel slow ...

... you lay the invisible foundation of greatness. One habit at a time. One belief at a time. One morning at a time.

And while the world might not see it yet – you will start to *feel* it. You will feel the strength forming. The resolve hardening. The inner scaffolding preparing to support the life you're about to step into.

Because when the time comes – and your breakthrough arrives – you'll rise fast. You'll rise strong. You'll rise sustainably. Not by chance. Not by luck. But because you were growing all along. Even when it feels slow. Even when results feel distant. Even when others say, "It's not working." Trust the process. Trust the pace. Trust your new Mind Power.

"The day you plant the seed is not the day the fruit appears – it's the day you make a promise to your future self. The harvest comes to those who keep showing up."

James Vincent

Accelerate your Mind Power

Now let's talk about power itself. In physics: strength × speed = power.

For example, if you have strength 3 and speed 2, your power is 6. But if you raise both to 5, your power becomes 25. That's not incremental growth – that's a quantum leap. So, let's apply that equation to your mind:

- **Mental strength**: your resilience, focus and endurance
- **Mental speed**: your agility, problem-solving and sharp thinking
- **Mind Power**: mental strength × mental speed

MENTAL SPEED × MENTAL STRENGTH

= MIND POWER

Build both your mental strength and speed, and you become unstoppable. Next, we are going to look at what fires your mental speed. Your purpose.

Purpose clears the path. A clear path means less hesitation, less wasted energy and faster decisions. With purpose, your thinking sharpens, your reactions quicken and you move with reason. That's why purpose is the ultimate accelerator of mental speed.

Identify your purpose

If you don't know who you truly are – and what drives you – you'll forever chase goals that don't fit you.

The clearer your self-understanding, the more precise your actions. The more precise your actions, the greater your momentum. And the greater your momentum, the more unstoppable you become.

When you live aligned with your purpose, everything changes:

- You'll learn faster
- You'll act smarter
- You'll stay focused while others fall apart.

So, how do you find the right purpose for you? How do you identify if you are on the right path? You ask yourself these questions:

1. **What impact do I want to make?**
   Purpose always begins with contribution. Who or what do you want to help, improve or change?
2. **Who am I becoming?**
   Not just what you do, but who you are growing into. Your identity drives your actions.
3. **What do I stand for?**
   The values you refuse to compromise on. Your non-negotiables.
4. **What problem am I here to solve?**
   Every lasting purpose connects to solving a problem bigger than yourself.
5. **Where do I feel most alive?**
   Energy is a clue. Purpose rarely feels draining – it feels expansive, even when it's hard.
6. **What future am I willing to build, no matter the obstacles?**
   The vision that still pulls you forward when comfort or fear would hold you back.

FINDING MY PURPOSE

When I first sat with these questions, I realized my answers didn't fit the world I was in anymore. That's when my mentor, Professor Patrick Duffy, helped me see the bigger purpose that was waiting for me. I'll never forget the moment that changed everything for me.

I was at the top of my game in Olympic sport – working with elite athletes, travelling the world, doing work I'd once dreamed of. From the outside, I looked like I was winning. But inside? Something was shifting.

I started to feel a quiet restlessness. I couldn't explain it. The passion was still there, but the purpose felt like it was fading. I was growing, but hitting a ceiling I couldn't ignore.

I sat down with Professor Duffy – former CEO of Sports Coach UK and President of the International Council of Coaching Excellence. He was the kind of man who could see deeper into you than you could see yourself. I'll never forget what he said:

"James ... maybe there's nothing wrong with you. Maybe you have a bigger purpose."

That line hit me like lightning. I realized I wasn't broken – I was misaligned. I was trying to grow a global vision that wasn't the perfect fit for me. That conversation became the turning point. I made the decision to leave elite sport – not because I was running from it, but because I was finally ready to grow beyond it. I chose to plant myself somewhere new. Somewhere rich with possibility.

That new direction was business coaching. A global platform. No ceiling. Real-world impact. And a vision – ActionCOACH – that matched the scale of my ambition.

And once I made the move ... everything grew. My work. My mindset. My mission. I'll always be grateful to Professor Duffy. He helped me see what I couldn't see on my own – that your purpose is everything.

What kind of performer are you?

Let's take a moment now to be honest with yourself. There are six types of people when it comes to performance, and knowing which one you are – right now – is the first step to transformation.

The Deadwood (very low potential, very low performance)
This is where growth goes to die. Deadwood drifts – disengaged, unskilled and uninterested. They aren't looking to improve, and they resist change. Whether from burnout, entitlement or complacency, they've mentally checked out. And when left in an organization, they quietly erode the culture.

If this is you: it's time for a wake-up call. You're not stuck – you're stagnant. Reignite your curiosity or find a new mission. Choose discomfort and growth over decay.

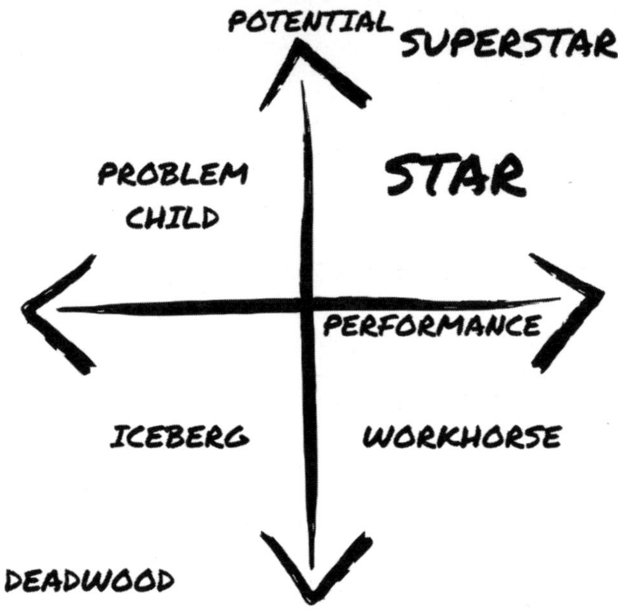

The six types of performer, based on potential and performance.

The Iceberg (low potential, low performance)

This person appears unmotivated and under-skilled. But don't be fooled – hidden beneath the surface is raw, untapped potential. They just haven't found the right environment to thrive in. Like an iceberg, one degree of change can either melt them ... or grow them.

If this is you, ask yourself: *What conditions bring out my best?* Your goal is to seek or create the right environment for you, deliberately.

The Workhorse (low potential, high performance)

These individuals have tremendous work ethic, and grind with everything they've got. They're in early, out late, and never complain about hard work. But they lack the right skills to move up.

If you're here: it's time to get smart. Upskill yourself. Don't become a slave to effort – become a master of leverage and upskill in the areas that will ensure you grow. Set aside time for planning ... give yourself direction, and plan where you are going. Even a simple plan will lift your potential and alleviate the instinct of "do more", "work harder" and "put more hours in". Increase skills, and plan!

The Problem Child (high potential, low performance)

They've got the talent but not the drive. They know what to do, but avoid doing it. Left unchecked, they drain teams and derail missions.

If this sounds like you – or someone you manage – don't enable the excuses. Raise the standard. Make accountability non-negotiable and develop your why. This person needs two things too ... the carrot and the stick. The stick is accountability, and the carrot is the why. Why do you want to be a performer?

The Star (high potential, high performance)
This person is a force of nature. Everyone wants to be a star. They execute with excellence and push consistently toward greatness. They're rare and powerful.

If you identify as this person: don't coast. Seek mentorship, structure and strategy to magnify your impact. You've only scratched the surface of your potential. Start focusing on bringing the right people around you, to guide you, challenge you, coach you. Maintaining a growth trajectory, being fuelled by purpose and being surrounded by people that challenge you is what's required.

The Superstar (very high potential, very high performance)
Superstars bring both elite talent and relentless drive over sustained long periods. A lot of people believe these superstars are "Unicorns", which is not the case – many find superstardom through being a star for more than ten years.

Superstars don't just meet expectations – they redefine them. They're visionaries *and* executors, capable of lifting entire teams with them. But beware: even stars burn out or stagnate without challenge.

If you're here: protect your Edge. Surround yourself with people who stretch you. You may need several coaches in several areas, because your sustained progression requires you to pursue hard problems, bigger stakes and higher purpose. You've got the Edge. Now make it the Infinite Edge.

***

Here's what matters: You **are not stuck** in one of these boxes. You are not a fixed character in a prewritten script. You are the writer.

Ask yourself these questions:

- What environments make me show up as my best self?
- What people energize me – and what people drain me?
- What habits make me stronger – and which ones shrink me?
- What problem am I solving that adds value?

Your answers will reveal more about who you really are. Be honest with yourself as you identify your performance type and know that you can be a Star or a Superstar when you harness the power of your mind and commit to the future you deserve.

"WHO DO YOU THINK YOU ARE?" EXERCISE

Identity drives behaviour. This is a truth most people miss. They focus on what to *do*, but not on who they are *being*. And this is why this matters:

- If you see yourself as weak, you'll give up early.
- If you see yourself as unlucky, you won't expect to win.
- If you see yourself as a creator, a leader, a driver of outcomes – you'll act accordingly.

So, who do you believe yourself to be in five words? Write them down, now.

- Then put "I am" before each of those words ...
- Then after each of your chosen five words, add "So I" and then add a meaning to the words. For example ... "I am inspirational ... So I light up the room wherever I go".
- Complete the five sentences and feel yourself rise mentally.
- Your next challenge is to act accordingly ...

Recognize how to grow

Knowing who you are today is only half the puzzle. The other half is knowing what you need to *grow further*:

- Some people need quiet. Others need chaos.
- Some need structure. Others need spontaneity.
- Some people recharge alone. Others recharge in connection.

There is no one-size-fits-all strategy for mental excellence. There is only what works for you. Most people never pause long enough to find out what really drives them or allows them to thrive. They follow the pack or routines from podcasts or gurus and wonder why they still feel unfulfilled. They chase goals that don't align with their wiring and then beat themselves up for falling short. Don't make that mistake.

Your job is to study *yourself*. Understand your rhythms. Reverse-engineer your highs – think about what makes you focused. Energized? Confident? And the opposite – what derails you?

For example:

- You might thrive as a *solo athlete*, where full control sharpens your focus – or you might perform better in a *team environment*, where energy and accountability lift you higher.
- You might love *writing in silence*, but after a while feel drained by isolation – which tells you to build in more human interaction.
- Some people find they do their best work *early in the morning*, when the world is quiet. Others don't hit their stride until *late at night*, once the day has settled.
- You might feel energized by *tight deadlines and pressure*, or discover you do your best work with *more space and reflection time.*
- Perhaps you recharge through *movement and activity* … or maybe it's stillness, reflection and rest that refuels you.

The point is: there are no right answers. The key is to notice what fuels you and what drains you – then design your environment and habits to match.

EXERCISE: MY PERFORMANCE PREFERENCES

Complete the sentence below by selecting the preferences in the list overleaf that most resonate with you. Circle one preference per line. Then fill out the sentences in the summary section.

In order to get the best out of myself, my preferences are …

Preference A	**Preference B**
Working independently	Working collaboratively
Exercising alone	Exercising with others
Relaxing in solitude	Relaxing socially
Short bursts of deep work	Long, sustained focus sessions
Focusing on one thing	Switching across multiple tasks
A fast, intense schedule	A calm, steady rhythm
Clear structure and predictability	Flexibility and spontaneity
Tight deadlines for pressure	Longer deadlines for reflection
Careful reflection before acting	Quick, decisive action
Quiet, distraction-free environment	Energetic, stimulating environment
Dim, calm lighting	Bright, energizing lighting
Physical activity to recharge	Mental stimulation to recharge
Routine and repetition	Variety and change
External accountability (team, coach)	Internal accountability (self-driven)
Competing to win	Improving to grow
Following proven systems	Experimenting with new ideas
Working with facts and logic	Working with vision and imagination
Taking deliberate recovery time	Pushing through discomfort
Seeking mastery in one skill	Developing breadth across skills

Summary: my winning conditions

When I perform at my best, I notice that I prefer …

- I focus best when …
- I work best with …
- I recharge through …
- I stay motivated by …
- I grow fastest when …

Now it's your responsibility to create these conditions daily. Make it happen.

Take a moment now to complete this exercise, to work out how you operate best:

Think of your identity and needs as your "inner operating system". If it's outdated, glitchy or misaligned, your performance will stall, no matter how hard you try. But when it's clear, current and calibrated, everything runs smoother.

That's the real work of inner alignment: calibration. Not wishful thinking. Not motivational fluff. But clear-eyed awareness of who you are and what unlocks your brilliance.

Find the right environment for you

If you put yourself in the Iceberg or Deadwood section earlier, you're not lazy, broken or stuck. More often than not, you're just in the wrong environment for you. You're in the wrong job, chasing the wrong goals, or using strategies that don't suit your nature. Change that – and you change everything.

Because when you know who you are and where you thrive, you stop trying to force results. You start generating them. That's the power of "aligned identity". Part of developing your Infinite Edge is to lift your potential higher and drive your performance further. Potential will increase your speed. Performance will increase your strength. Together these will develop Mind Power. That's the beginning of unstoppable momentum.

If you're a Star or Superstar, then you don't have it easy either. The better you get, the more challenging it is to get better. Long-term sustained execution, marginal gains and strategy can take you further. This is where flow comes in, and that's up next.

Find your flow

If you've ever written for hours without noticing the clock, if you've ever played, worked, created or led with total presence, then you've felt it. You've experienced flow, also known as a flow state. You know its power – a mental state so transformative that once you've experienced flow – truly entered it – you'll wonder how you ever lived without it. The goal is not to get into the flow state every now and again, but to stay in it for long, sustained periods, even infinitely.

You can be talented and still stuck. You can be smart and still scattered. You can be dedicated and still drained. Why? Because talent and hard work without flow is like a sports car without fuel. It looks good, but it doesn't move.

You weren't born for burnout or disconnection. As a child, you knew flow well. You lived in it. You *played* in it. You painted with wild abandon and lost hours in imagination. You didn't measure productivity – you measured joy. That version of you isn't gone. It's simply been buried – under stress, fear, noise and competition.

So, how do you get that incredible Mind Power back?

Here's the truth most people never hear: flow is not a fluke. Flow is not a gift. Flow is a *skill*. A trainable, repeatable, engineerable skill – and one that unlocks your Mind Power: the state where your potential meets its performance. Where greatness doesn't feel like a stretch, but a *standard*.

When you understand the mechanics of flow, you don't have to wait for it. You *build* it. You *summon* it. You live in it by design, not by accident.

Why flow gives you the Edge

In his masterpiece *Flow: The Psychology of Happiness*, psychologist Mihaly Csikszentmihalyi explains that flow is not the privilege of the elite – it is the right of every human being willing to engage fully. Those who live in flow:

- Are more productive
- Feel more meaning in their work
- Experience deeper happiness – not because life is perfect, but because they are fully *present* in it. Happiness is not found in the outcome – but in the *immersion*.

Flow doesn't require special conditions. It requires complete involvement in whatever you're doing. It arises when your skill meets the perfect level

WHAT DOES FLOW FEEL LIKE?

Flow is the highest expression of human focus.

- Psychologists call it "the zone".
- Athletes call it "being locked in".
- Artists say they're "being moved by something greater".

Whatever the term, the experience is the same:

- You lose track of time.
- You act without overthinking.
- You deliver your best work with ease.
- You feel *energized* – not drained – even after hours of effort.
- You don't just perform – you *transcend*.

And the most miraculous part? Flow isn't rare. It isn't mystical. It's *repeatable*.

of challenge. When your attention merges with your intention. When your whole self shows up to the moment at hand.

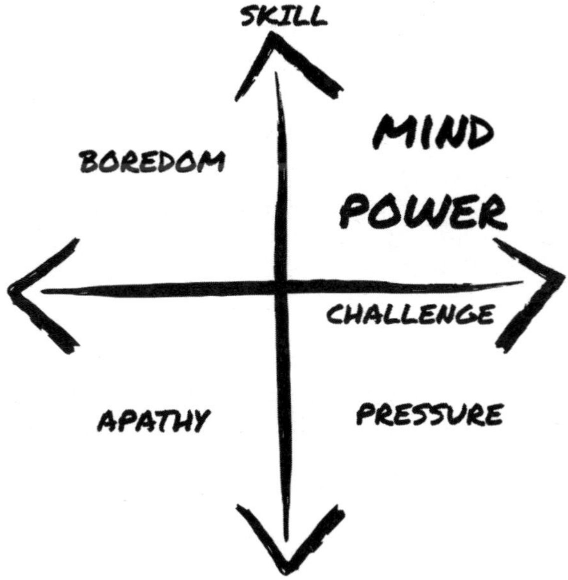

Mind Power lives at the intersection of high skill and high challenge. Stay here – and you'll grow, flow and perform at your best.

Train your mind for flow

> *"The best moments usually occur when a person's body or mind is stretched to its limits in a voluntary effort to accomplish something difficult and worthwhile."*
>
> Mihaly Csikszentmihalyi

Every time your mind is focused on a challenge just beyond your current capability, you become more of who you're meant to be. This is the core of flow – your brain becomes fully engaged. And then *flow grows you.*

Let me give you an example. Rico worked on an assembly line for five years doing the same task, yet loved it. Why? He turned it into a game. He timed each unit he built, kept a personal record, and tried to beat it. What would have driven others mad, gave him flow. His mind wasn't trapped – it was engaged.

What's blocking your flow?

Take a moment to think about your goals, your work, your training. Do you feel in flow when you work toward your goals? What's blocking you? Let's look at the four inner mental blocks that stand between you and your peak flow performance and, importantly, how to overcome them:

1. Apathy

This is when you feel flat and unmotivated. It's not that you're lazy – you feel apathy because you've lost sight of why your effort matters. To destroy apathy, you must reconnect with your purpose. Ask yourself:

- Why does this matter?
- Who will benefit if I do well or win?
- Who might suffer if I stop?

Purpose turns a simple task into a mission. And when you remember the *why*, you unlock the *will.*

2. Boredom

The silent killer of momentum, boredom sneaks in when your skills far outpace the challenge. Tasks feel beneath you, so you disengage. You coast, you scroll. But boredom isn't a sign to stop – it's a sign to stretch. Here's how to reignite your enthusiasm:

- **Add a creative constraint** – for example, set yourself a rule to give a presentation with only five slides instead of 20, or write an article in exactly 500 words. Boundaries like these force your brain to think differently and spark new ideas.
- **Shorten your timeline** – give yourself half the usual time and see how sharp your focus becomes.
- **Raise your personal standards** – aim for excellence, not just completion.
- **Push the boundaries just enough to wake up your mind** – step outside your comfort zone, but not so far that you freeze.

And flow will find its way back to you.

3. Pressure

This doesn't just block flow – it *buries* it. When the challenge feels too big and your skill feels too small, panic creeps in. You freeze. You doubt. You retreat. The key here is to break down the task:

- Split the mountain into molehills.
- Shrink the task until it becomes conquerable – then conquer the first step.
- That first win creates momentum.

And that momentum can lead you into flow.

4. Distraction

Even the slightest interruption can eject you from flow like a faulty ejector seat. A ping from your phone. A scroll. A stray thought. Suddenly you're out of the moment. To protect your flow, build your fortress:

- Focus on one task at a time.
- Use one screen – put all other screens out of sight.
- Aim for one clear outcome.

The world may reward multitasking – but flow demands your full attention.

How to stay in flow

Flow doesn't happen by luck. It happens by *structure*. Here's a practical method to help you enter, stay in and return to flow as often as you choose:

1. **Connect to your purpose**. Before you start your task or training, ask yourself: *Why does this matter?* Link the task to a mission, outcome or future self that excites you. Passion fuels persistence.
2. **Set a clear goal**. Know what success looks like before you begin. Write it down and be specific. Vague goals equal vague energy.
3. **Eliminate distractions.** Silence your notifications. Clear your work or performance space. Focus is sacred.
4. **Challenge your skill.** Aim for the edge of your ability. Your task or goal should not be too easy or too hard. Just sharp enough to stretch you.
5. **Use time blocks.** Work in deep, focused sprints of 45–90 minutes. Then rest. Rhythm over grind.
6. **Reflect and reward.** Celebrate what you achieved. Reflection solidifies learning and builds motivation for the next round.

This ritual is your launchpad. Repeat it often enough, and your mind will *expect* flow. You'll no longer chase it – you'll *live* in it.

FLOW AND INFINITE EDGE

When you master flow:

- Your stress decreases
- Your performance multiplies
- Your joy returns.

And success becomes *a rhythm*, not a random spark. This is the zone where mastery is born. This is where you find your Infinite Edge. Where ordinary people create extraordinary things.

And the more you live in flow, the more you align with the person you were *always meant to be*.

EFFORTLESS FLOW

Annie didn't look like the strongest player on court. She wasn't the tallest. She wasn't the most physically imposing. At first glance, you might even underestimate her.

And then the match would start.

From the first rally, she moved with a calm, almost effortless rhythm. Where her opponents strained and fought for every shot, Annie glided. Her racket control was razor-sharp, her timing immaculate, and her focus unshakable. It looked so smooth, so natural, that people often mistook it for ease. But I knew better.

Behind that flow was years of practice. Hours of skill-building, deliberate repetition and mental composure. What unlocked it wasn't brute force – it was the right foundation of fitness. When Annie had her physical base in place, she could slip into that state where the game slowed down, and everything just clicked.

I remember watching her dismantle top European players, not by overpowering them, but by outmaneuvering them. While they fought with muscle, she played with mind, skill and calmness. She made world-class opponents look ordinary because she was playing in flow – and they weren't.

The lesson was clear: strength and power can take you far, but they won't take you all the way. Flow beats force, if you know how to create it.

That's the paradox of high performance. The harder you push, the tighter you grip, the more mistakes creep in. But when you've done the work – when your skills are sharp, your focus is clear, and your body has its base – you can let go. You can play free. That's when performance becomes poetry.

Principle: True Performance Edge isn't about being the biggest or the strongest. It's about mastering your skills, calming your mind, and finding that state of flow where your best feels effortless.

"Your greatest moments live at the edge of your ability – where pressure meets purpose and you rise to meet both."

James Vincent

In summary, flow doesn't come from trying harder. It comes from clear purpose and challenges that stretch – not snap – you. This is how your Mind Power builds momentum. This is how you build your Edge.

Performance psychology: understand yourself

Even with the best environment, and the clearest goals, you can still struggle if what's happening *inside* you is at war. You don't grow just by working harder – you grow by building the right relationships *within yourself*.

This section is about examining those parts of yourself that govern your focus, your thoughts and, ultimately, your destiny. They operate in the background, whispering through your self-talk, guiding your decisions and tugging at your confidence – often without you knowing (*see* Your subconscious: the silent operator, page 14).

I had to stop chasing performance and start understanding myself before I could move forward. So, here's where you start facing what's holding you back. You need to examine your:

- Past
- Future
- Present

Each can be your greatest ally or your silent saboteur. Each can anchor you in place or elevate you to greatness. Let's explore them, one by one:

Your past

The past is not just a place you came from. It's the lens through which you see your life today. Your memories, mistakes, wins and wounds don't stay back there in the past. They live inside you. They drive how you react under pressure. They shape the limits you place on yourself. They become the blueprint for how you think you're "supposed" to be.

But let this truth sink in: *the past is not your prison – it is your platform.* And when you learn to stand on it, instead of in it, everything changes.

You cannot grow while looking backward in regret. But you can rise by looking back with purpose. To master your past, follow these two rules:

Rule 1: Learn from your past

The past is not a place to punish yourself – stop playing your lowlights like a greatest hits album. Stop turning your failures into a life sentence. Instead, ask yourself the golden question: *What was life trying to teach me?* Extract the patterns. Spot the lessons. Distil the wisdom. A painful past is not a sign of weakness – it is the start of a winning future.

Rule 2: Draw strength from your past

You are still standing, and that's no small thing. There are chapters of your story that could have broken you, but they didn't. Why? Because resilience lives in your roots.

Confidence isn't built by pretending life was easy. It's built by *remembering what you've survived* – and choosing to honour it. You've already proven yourself in the face of storms. Now, let that history become your inner roar.

You are not your past. But your past – if you use it wisely – can become the power behind your present. Your mind is not there to beat you, it's there to build you.

Your future

There are two ways of looking into the future ... one is with worry and the other is with optimism. The future is not a threat – it's an invitation. The Edge you grow today is shaped by the future you expect tomorrow.

And yet, most people fear the future. They freeze. And in doing so, they surrender their power *before they even begin.*

Here is the truth: the future does not create you. *You* create the future. But only if you approach it with clarity, not confusion.

Start with intention. Intention is the spark that turns chaos into creation. It's not just a wish or a dream – it's a decision. A decision to meet tomorrow with boldness. To point your life in a deliberate direction and say: "That's where I'm going. That's who I'm becoming."

When you move with intention, something magical happens: Fear fades. Energy rises. And you begin to act like a builder, not a bystander. People with plans move differently. They speak with conviction. They act with precision. Why? Because they've already visited the future in their mind. Planning doesn't guarantee perfection, but it does create momentum.

When you take the time to map the road ahead:

- You make fewer detours
- You build your day with discipline
- You stop drifting and start deciding.

And here's the most powerful part: the moment you start shaping the future, the future starts shaping you.

I didn't always understand this. In fact, there was a time when my relationship with the future nearly broke me. I was young and competing at national and international level. I was driven, trained, focused. But before the big competitions, I'd freeze. Not physically ... mentally.

I wasn't scared of my opponent. I wasn't scared of losing. I was scared of the future. My thoughts spiralled – what if I failed? What if I wasn't good enough? What if everything I'd worked for crumbled on court in front of everyone?

I didn't realize it back then, but my relationship with the future was broken. I was imagining disaster, not victory. I was running mental rehearsals for failure. And my thoughts? They were sabotaging me before the match had even begun.

But at some point – and I don't remember the exact moment – I snapped out of it. I made a shift. I stopped feeding worry and started feeding preparation. I reprogrammed every doubt into a direction. My mind stopped being the obstacle and became the advantage.

That's the moment I learned the truth: your mind isn't fixed. It's programmable. I'm the programmer of my future. And you are too.

Your present

The present isn't just where you live – it's where you grow. The present is the only moment that gives you power. The past is gone. The future is imagined. But the present? That's where confidence is built and momentum begins. As Eckhart Tolle explained:

> *"Realize deeply that the present moment is all you ever have. Make the Now the primary focus of your life."*

Most people misunderstand time. They live in reaction to the past or anticipation of the future. But successful people learn to return again and again to the now. Why? Because the present is the only place where your thoughts become action. And action is the birthplace of confidence, clarity and results.

As the wise words from Kung Fu Panda remind us:

> *"Yesterday is history. Tomorrow is a mystery. But today is a gift ... that's why they call it the present."*

***

You can't enter flow while your mind is scattered. You can't build belief while distracted. You can't lead others if you're not present with yourself.

To master the present is to master your Edge. It is to slow down in the moments that matter, eliminate distractions, feel deeply and choose intentionally. It is to do what you're doing with *all* of you – not just the scraps of focus left over after a scroll through your notifications.

Presence isn't passivity. It's Mind Power. Don't drift. Direct. Channel your energy with intent – here, now, on purpose.

In high performance, presence is everything. It's how you enter flow. It's how you show up with full energy. It's how you catch the small wins that stack into momentum. That's why eliminating distractions, challenging your skill in real time and setting clear goals are the keys to sustained excellence. As Brendon Burchard teaches:

> *"Self-mastery is full presence. It's joy, it's confidence, it's a positive range of our psychology that makes us have reverence for the moment so now we can dance together."*

So be here. All in. Today. That's where your Infinite Edge sharpens.

Celebration

There is a fourth, bonus relationship with yourself I want to talk about. *Celebration.*

When you celebrate your successes, it energizes you, strengthens your belief and teaches your subconscious: "*This is who I am.*"

Every time you acknowledge a win, big or small, you teach your mind: "*Success is normal. Progress is who I am.*"

That's not self-indulgence – that's strategy. Most people think celebration is about ego. It's not – it's about reinforcement and identity. Celebration is sunlight for your Edge.

When you celebrate, your life becomes a series of upward spirals, each one stronger than the last. That's how your Edge evolves: not just through striving – but through honouring the progress. What you celebrate becomes part of your default programming.

Celebration is, perhaps, the most overlooked relationship with ourselves. And yet it holds the key to sustainable motivation, emotional resilience and inner peace. Because what you celebrate, you reinforce. And what you reinforce – you repeat.

THE GREEN PEN MOMENT

Let's look now at how you can get into the habit of celebrating yourself (because my guess is, some of you don't do this anywhere often enough).

When you hit a goal, don't just move on. Celebrate it. Out loud. In full colour. Grab a green pen right now – the colour of growth – and put a bold tick next to that goal you wrote down (see page 36). If you don't have a written record of your goal, then make one now, as a permanent memento of your achievement. And don't forget to give it that green tick. Make it ceremonial. Let yourself feel it. Say out loud: *"Yes. I did that."*

Let that win land. Let it anchor. Let it signal to your system:

- "This is who I'm becoming."
- "I did it."
- "I am successful."
- "I make things happen."
- "I am a winner."

Celebrate with others

You didn't climb this mountain alone. So, when you win, let others win with you. Pop the cork. Buy the cake. Bring the moment home. Tell your family, loved ones, coaches, colleagues, teammates, band members, customers, clients, community: *"We're moving forward. We did it. This is for us."*

THE POWER TO CHOOSE

Before we close, let me give you one of the most powerful demonstrations of Mind Power I've ever come across.

It's the story of Viktor Frankl – a respected neurologist and psychiatrist, and a man who lost everything during the Holocaust. His home. His family. His freedom. Even his name. In the brutal silence of the Nazi concentration camps, Frankl found himself stripped to nothing but thought.

But it was in that space – the space between what happened to him and how he responded – that he discovered the greatest Mind Power: the power to choose. He wrote:

"Between stimulus and response, there is a space. In that space is our power to choose our response. In our response lies our growth and our freedom."

Surrounded by starvation, cruelty and death, Frankl realized something profound: the Nazis could control his outer world, but never his inner one. They could imprison his body – but not his identity. They could not dictate his thoughts. They could not own his meaning.

So he chose purpose. He chose to believe that his pain could be transformed into teaching. That his survival could become service. That suffering – if met with meaning – could become strength.

He began asking fellow prisoners a powerful question: "What do you want from life when you get out of here?"

This question gave people hope. And hope gave them energy. It shifted their focus from despair to direction. Frankl imagined himself standing on a stage one day, teaching others about the psychology of survival. And that image – that vision – pulled him through hell.

Even when he learned that his wife had died, he made a choice. Not to give up. Not to harden. But to hold onto her memory as a source of love and strength. That decision saved him.

Frankl's story isn't just about survival. It's about the ultimate truth of Mind Power: you always have a choice. You may not control what happens, but you control what it means. And the meaning you choose, becomes the mind you build.

If Viktor Frankl could find meaning in the unimaginable, what might you find in your next challenge?

Because celebration doesn't just honour the moment – it reminds you why the journey matters. It teaches your mind to crave progress with joy, not pressure. And it inspires everyone around you to do the same.

A new you

When these elements of yourself (past, future, present and celebration) are in harmony, life no longer feels like a grind – it becomes a rhythm. You stop wrestling with yourself and start working *with* yourself. You become the person who:

- Learns fast
- Plans wisely
- Acts boldly
- Celebrates generously.

And in doing so in your life, true transformation takes hold. Not overnight or by accident, but through the conscious mastering of the relationship with yourself that shapes every thought, action and outcome of your life.

Final thought: mastering your Mind Power

You've just taken the first step toward mastering the most powerful tool you will ever possess – your mind.

You are not your background. Not your circumstances. Not your education, talent or connections. You are your *mind.*

And now you know what most people never discover: your mind has a *purpose.* It is not fixed. It is a force – and you are its commander. From this point forward, let these truths echo within you:

- You are not trapped. You are not broken. You are not too late.
- You are becoming. You are capable. You are powerful beyond measure.

And the best is yet to come.

FORCE 2
THE CONFIDENCE LOOP

"Thoughts build belief, and belief builds everything that follows."

James Vincent

In the last chapter, you learned to harness your Mind Power – the roots beneath the surface. But even the strongest roots can't grow into a tree if the soil above them is crowded with weeds. And those weeds? They are self-doubt. They crowd out momentum and block self-belief from rising. So, in this chapter we are going to look at how to clear those weeds and instead grow confidence.

Confidence doesn't grow by luck. It's not talent. It's not something you stumble into. Confidence is a force inside you – one you consciously build, brick by brick, choice by choice. It's the inner fuel that turns preparation into performance. The voice in your head can be your greatest enemy, but when trained, it becomes the biggest performance enhancer in the world.

Confidence in your system is like oxygen in your lungs – invisible, but vital to life and performance. It's what allows you to breathe under pressure, move with conviction and keep going when others crumble. Without it, your potential stays buried. With it, your Edge comes alive.

That's where the Confidence LOOP comes in. It's a psychological routine – a set of repeatable inner actions that gives confidence a place to live. It's the system that clears space, repels self-doubt and allows self-belief to rise.

Because self-doubt will always creep in – that's being human. When your self-belief is weak, you start second-guessing your instincts. You rely on other people's approval to act. You pull back from moments that matter. You wait. And in that waiting, doubt returns.

The Confidence LOOP allows your self-confidence to emerge – not by magic, but by deliberate mental actions, in the right order, at the right time:

LOOP = Let go of doubt → Open to belief → Own belief → Plant belief

Let's break that down:

Let go of doubt

Doubt is human. It will show up, but it doesn't need to take root. Letting go isn't denial – it's a decision to stop entertaining thoughts that don't serve you. So take one of your doubts right now and stop holding onto it. Let it go.

Open to belief

Once you've released doubt, you've cleared mental space. But nature – and the mind – hates a vacuum. What you fill that space with matters. This is your chance to lean into possibility – not fake positivity or forced hype, but openness. A willingness to say: "Maybe I can." "Maybe this is possible." That tiny crack of belief? That's where confidence begins.

Own belief

Now that belief has sparked, you must claim it. Don't wait to feel "ready". Don't look around for proof. Own it. Declare it yours, before the world validates it. This act of ownership is internal. It builds autonomy. It strengthens your identity. And it rewires your system to trust itself again. Confidence isn't gifted – it's claimed. And owning belief is how that claim is made.

Plant belief

Now self-belief becomes rooted. You embed it into your mental soil so it can grow. This is the final – and most overlooked – step. Because if belief isn't planted, it's forgotten. But if it is planted? It matures. It multiplies.

"HAVE BELIEF"

Let me tell you a story. One that changed my life – and showed me what belief really means.

I was nine years old. My family had just brought home a little Jack Russell puppy named Sam. He was energetic, wild and my absolute best friend. One day, I took him for a walk to the park. As we approached, he wriggled free from his collar ... and bolted.

In seconds, he was gone. I chased him, yelling his name, panic rising with every step. He darted toward the main road. I couldn't keep up. The world blurred. My heart was thumping. All I could think was, "What if I lose him forever?"

I turned a corner ... and heard the screech of tyres. Breath gone. Legs trembling. I thought the worst. I ran home, eyes full of tears, burst into the house and cried out to my dad, "Sam's gone. I can't find him!"

My dad knelt down, looked me in the eyes and said five words I'll never forget:

"Have belief. You'll find him."

That was it. No panic. Just calm certainty. And in that moment ... something shifted. The fear started to fade. I stopped chasing in chaos. I breathed. I believed. I turned around to head back – and there he was. Right behind me. Tail wagging. As if nothing had happened. I knelt down and hugged him, tears running freely. But this wasn't just relief ... it was a lesson I'd never forget:

Belief doesn't mean certainty. It means calm in chaos. It means being open to the idea that things will come good – even when you can't see how.

EXERCISE: THE LOOP BUILDER

You've seen how the LOOP works. Now it's time to run it yourself. This exercise will help you build self-belief deliberately – not by chance, but by practice.

Do this at the start of each day:

1. Let go of doubt
   Write down 1–2 doubts holding you back. Then cross them out.
   Example: "I'm not ready."
2. Open to belief
   Replace them with one possibility.
   Example: "Maybe I can deliver a clear version today."
3. Own belief
   Claim your identity in the present tense. Say it out loud.
   Example: "I belong in this room."
4. Plant belief
   Prove it with one small action today.
   Example: "I'll send the first draft before lunch."

At the end of the day, log one proof: "*Today I proved my belief when ...*"

Now say this affirmation:

"*Trust yourself, [NAME]. You've planted belief – and it will grow.*"

The LOOP isn't a one-time reset – it's a rhythm. Each time you run it, you turn belief into action, and action into evidence. That evidence becomes self-trust, and self-trust is the root of lasting confidence.

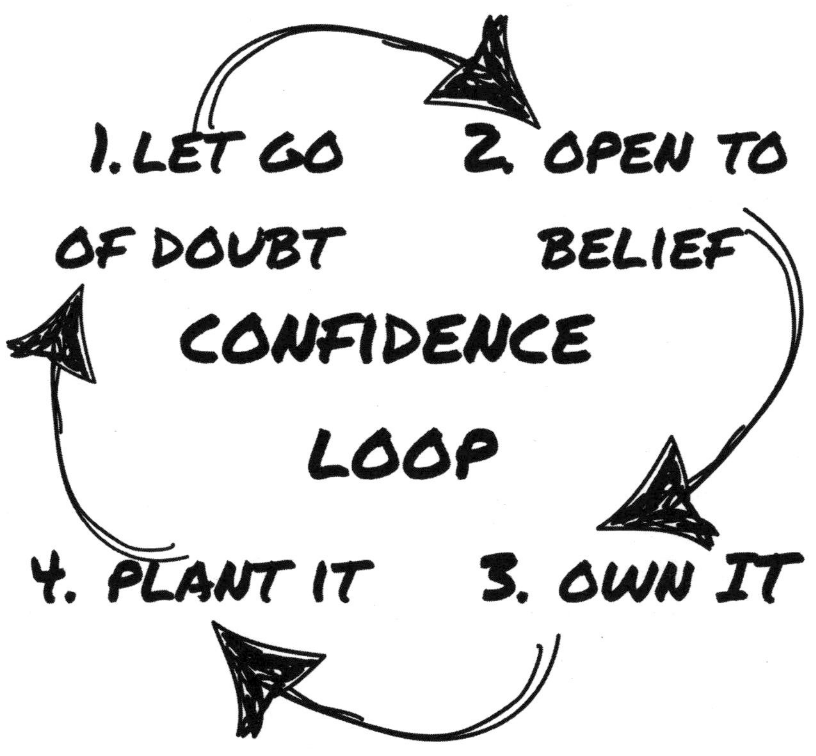

Confidence isn't a gift – it's a cycle. Let go of doubt, open to belief, own it and plant it ... then run the LOOP again.

Confidence is intention

Doubt will always return – in different forms, in different seasons. The question is never: "Will I doubt?" The question is: "What will I feed?"

A young boy once sat with his grandfather and said: "Grandpa, sometimes I feel full of fear and self-doubt. But other times, I feel strong, like I believe in myself. Why does that happen?"

The grandfather nodded slowly and replied: "That's because there are two wolves inside us all. One is full of fear, doubt, hesitation and shame. The other is full of belief, love, courage and strength. And those two wolves ... they're always fighting."

The boy thought for a moment. "Which one wins?"

The grandfather smiled. "The one you feed."

That's the power of the LOOP. It's how you choose which wolf gets stronger. It's how you feed belief – and starve doubt. Every time you run the LOOP, you let go of doubt and open to belief. You own it. You plant it.

You reinforce the belief that shapes your future. Because confidence doesn't grow automatically. It grows by *intention*. Feed doubt, and it takes over. Feed belief, and your future expands.

This is not a one-time reset – it's a lifelong system. Every time you run this LOOP, you stop self-doubt from stealing your future. The LOOP is how confidence builds – not in bursts, but in rhythm. Not in feelings, but in force. Confidence is not just a feeling – it's a force you build, run and plant – again and again.

What confidence looks like

Once belief is planted, something beautiful begins to rise. A quiet strength. A solidness in who you are and who you're becoming. That's self-belief. That's confidence.

Not a passing thought, not a motivational burst, but a *core conviction* – earned, strengthened and reinforced by looping belief back into your system. You can start to tell yourself:

- "I don't need to be perfect – just ready."
- "This is my moment. I've earned it."
- "I'll figure it out."
- "I trust myself to act, not overthink."

This isn't bravado or arrogance. It's a quiet inner-knowing that says: "I've looped belief enough to know I belong, I deserve this chance and I can do it."

And you'll know confidence is real when it shows up in the moments that matter most.

For an athlete, it's standing on the starting line, heart racing, crowd roaring – and that quiet inner voice says: *"I've done the work. I belong here. Let's go."*

For a CEO, it's walking into the boardroom with investors waiting. Pressure sky-high. Instead of shrinking, they step forward: *"I know this business inside out. I trust my decisions. They need me to lead."*

For a parent, it's being at their child's hospital bedside. Fear could take over, but confidence whispers: *"I can stay calm. I can make the right calls. My child needs my strength right now."*

For one of my clients – let's call her Sarah – it was public speaking. At first, just the thought of standing on stage froze her. But by running the LOOP – planting belief, rehearsing action, trusting herself – she went from panic to presence. Today, she speaks to 200+ staff without notes.

And for me, I'll never forget standing backstage at a global conference, about to speak to thousands. Doubt rushed in, but I'd looped belief enough times to tell myself: *"You've earned this moment. Deliver. It's not about you James ... it's all about them. Enjoy."* And I did.

The point is this: none of these moments are accidents. They're the result of looping belief into action, again and again, until it becomes automatic. That's the power of the LOOP – it builds the kind of confidence that doesn't disappear under pressure, but doubles down when you need it most.

Your confidence becomes visible. It reaches into your work, your relationships, your leadership, your creativity and your life:

- You take action without needing validation.
- You speak without shrinking.
- You move forward without guarantees.
- You recover faster when doubt creeps back in.

These are the real-time expressions of inner belief, lived out loud. They don't grow by luck. They grow through repetition, through principle, through pressure. And each one is a force of confidence.

Courage – confidence in motion

"You'll never feel like it. But act anyway."

– Mel Robbins, *The 5 Second Rule*

We've all felt that moment. The pause before you speak in a meeting. Before you step onto the stage. The breath you hold before asking the uncomfortable question. The rush of heat before raising your hand, clicking publish or making a call you're scared to make.

HOW TO BUILD COURAGE EVERY DAY

Courage is a muscle. It grows through repetition. And one way to train your courage is to use "micro-moments":

- Do one small scary thing daily: Send the message. Ask the question in the meeting. Say what you mean instead of staying silent. Raise your hand in class. Email the agent. Introduce yourself to a stranger.

Not every act of courage is life-changing – but every one is identity-shaping.

When you feel fear rising, say to yourself:

- "This is the moment I train my confidence."

Every act of courage is a deposit into your self-belief bank. You don't need to be bold all day. Just in the moments that matter. You may not feel brave. But the moment you act – you *become brave*.

Every time you step forward when standing still would be easier, you're telling your system: "This is who I am now."

Courage is that electric space between knowing what you could do – and deciding that you will. That's where confidence is earned. Not when you're fearless, but when you fear ... and still move forward.

Without courage, your confidence collapses at the moment of opportunity. You hold back. You shrink your voice. You start bargaining with your potential – "*Maybe later. Maybe when it's perfect. Maybe when I feel more sure.*" And each time you do that, your Confidence LOOP weakens. You reinforce hesitation. You train your system to wait. But confidence – real confidence – is motion. It needs to be lived. Repeated. Reinforced. And courage is the first breath that brings it to life.

Imagine standing at the edge of a high diving board. You're staring down. The water looks miles away. Your heart races, legs tremble, and voices swirl in your head. What if I fall wrong? What if I'm not ready? That moment – that Edge – is the real test. Not the jump itself. Not the landing. But *the decision to leap*. That's courage. It's the spark that turns hesitation into movement.

Waiting until you "feel ready" is a trap. If you're chasing the feeling of certainty before you act, you'll wait forever. Confidence lives in the quiet decision to do the hard thing anyway. So, how do you get more of it?

Being honest with yourself

If courage is what moves you forward, honesty is what keeps you aligned. Honesty is the part of you that says, "Let's look at what's really going on." Because confidence without honesty is fake. But confidence with honesty is power.

THE WINDOW OF GROWTH

Most people live behind a window – pointing at everything outside: blaming the boss, the timing, the market, the weather, their past. The truth is … you can't fix what's outside of you, anyway. But what's inside? That's yours to change.

We all have blind spots. We all carry parts of ourselves we'd rather avoid: patterns, weaknesses, habits and truths we don't want to face. But here's the thing:

You cannot grow from what you refuse to confront.

You cannot fix what you're unwilling to admit.

CHALLENGE YOURSELF: HOW HONEST ARE YOU?

Honesty starts quietly, and with questions. Take this moment to ask yourself:

- What's holding me back?
- Am I being consistent with what I say I want?
- Am I avoiding something I know I need to face?

- Am I living in alignment with the standards I claim to hold?

Most people won't attempt these questions, because the answers are uncomfortable. But confident people ask them anyway. Not because they like the answers, but because they're committed to becoming the person who can handle the truth. Write your real answers. No filters. No fluff. Just the truth.

You can also try this:

- Speak your honest truth to someone you trust. Say it out loud. Let it echo back.

When you live from the truth, when you ask better questions, face hard realities and hold yourself to a higher standard, you stop faking confidence. And you start living it.

THE STUCK COMPASS

Imagine trying to navigate your life with a compass that's off by 10 degrees. You won't notice it at first. But over time, you drift miles off course. Honesty is your recalibration tool. It realigns your internal compass, so your direction is clean, consistent and congruent. That's what confidence feeds on: congruence. A life where who you say you are and how you actually live are the same thing.

THE COST OF AVOIDING HONESTY

When you avoid honesty:

- You start lying to yourself – subtly, daily.
- You lower your standards to fit your current effort.
- You surround yourself with people who won't challenge you.
- And worst of all, you become someone you don't fully respect – even if no one else sees it.

THE WEALTH OF CHOOSING HONESTY

When you choose honesty:

- You upgrade your self-respect.
- You sharpen your clarity.
- You realign your actions with your potential.

Honesty is the light switch. It brings clarity to the corners of your character. It removes the fog between who you are ... and who you want to become.

When honesty is missing, you may appear strong to others, but inside, your confidence is hollow. Without honesty, you build your confidence on shaky ground – on image, not identity:

- You ignore your inconsistencies.
- You justify procrastination.
- You deflect accountability.
- You blame your circumstances instead of challenging yourself.

And every time you do that, your belief system erodes – not dramatically, but silently. One small lie at a time. Until one day you wake up and wonder why you feel so disconnected from your goals.

Honesty clears the fog. It reconnects you to reality – not to shame you, but to free you. Brené Brown expresses it best:

"Vulnerability is clarity. And clarity is strength."

THE DISCIPLINED COACH

Varvara Lewis wasn't just a coach. She was a standard to look up to.

Nobody turned up late for Varvara. Nobody. Because with her, lateness wasn't about traffic or excuses – it was about attitude. And attitude, in her world, was non-negotiable.

I remember athletes whispering before sessions: "You don't mess with Varvara." And they were right. She demanded discipline, structure and respect. But here's the thing – it wasn't fear that made people sharpen up. It was belief. Varvara carried herself with such conviction that you wanted to rise to her level.

Varvara had a gift for instilling one of the most underrated truths of performance: your habits reflect your character. If you're late, sloppy or half-committed, it isn't just about minutes on a clock – it's about the mindset you're bringing to the table.

Varvara drilled this into her badminton players until it became second nature. Discipline wasn't punishment; it was pride. Structure wasn't restriction; it was freedom.

And that's the legacy she left: not just athletes who could win matches, but people who carried integrity into everything they did.

Principle: Discipline is the root of integrity. When your standards are strong, your confidence has something to stand on.

CHALLENGE YOUR INTEGRITY

Most people say they have integrity – but integrity isn't what you claim, it's what you consistently do. Pause and test it for yourself. Use these prompts to reflect – and be honest in your answers:

- Do my actions change based on what others think of me?
- Do I act differently depending on how the day is going?
- Do I stay consistent when things aren't going my way?
- Do I keep or break promises to myself and others?
- Do I set goals but then fail to protect the time to make them happen?
- Do I talk about values but compromise them under pressure?
- Do I show up differently depending on who's in the room?

Write down one or two areas where your integrity slips. Then write the opposite – what it would look like to stay aligned.

Example 1 (athlete): Think of an athlete who commits to early-morning training. No cameras. No applause. Just them and the track. Every session they show up, they're not only building fitness – they're building confidence. Why? Because every time you keep a promise to yourself, you prove to your own mind that you can be trusted. And trust in yourself is the root of confidence.

Example 2 (business leader): Or picture a leader who tells their team, "*You'll have feedback by Friday.*" If they deliver every time, the team's trust deepens – and the leader's self-confidence grows too. But if they keep missing deadlines, both trust and self-respect erode. Confidence is built in exactly the same way: every kept promise adds to it, every broken one chips away at it.

Because every time you compromise, your confidence becomes a little harder to access. Not because you're incapable – but because you stop believing your own voice. Integrity isn't lost in one big moment. It's eroded in a thousand small ones where you said, "*I'll do it tomorrow.*"

COMMIT TO INTEGRITY

Write down 2–3 specific actions you will take to strengthen your integrity. These become your daily checks – the proof you're building trust with yourself.

1.

2.

3.

Every promise you keep is a mini Confidence LOOP. Each one feeds belief, starves doubt and builds the unshakable trust in yourself that confidence lives on.

WHAT INTEGRITY SOUNDS LIKE

Integrity is the invisible promise you make to your future self – and the discipline to keep it. It sounds like:

- "I said I'd do it – so I will."
- "This isn't easy, but it's right."
- "No one's watching – but I am."
- "I can trust myself to follow through."

That's what honesty is: strength. Not in perfection – but in presence. Because the moment you see things clearly, you can change them.

Integrity – confidence in character

Confidence is built on many things, but nothing holds it together like integrity. Integrity is about being consistent, reliable and aligned. It's what makes your confidence feel real, not rehearsed. Integrity is the part of you that doesn't sway when no one's watching.

It's easy to be confident when everything's going well, but the true test is who you are when it isn't. It's not about being flawless – no human being can be that, but integrity is your quiet commitment to act in alignment – even when no one's clapping. Integrity means:

- You can count on yourself.
- Your words match your actions.
- Your private decisions match your public standards.
- You say what you mean – and more importantly, you do what you say.

When you live with integrity, your confidence isn't conditional. It's consistent.

How to build integrity

Integrity is built like muscle, through repetition. It doesn't require perfection, just consistency. Start with micro-promises to yourself. For example:

- Wake when you say you will.
- Hit the gym when you planned. Drink the water. Send the message.
- Honour your own calendar. If it's in your diary, do it. Don't ghost your goals.
- Do the right thing – especially when it's hard.
- The moment you want to take the shortcut is the exact moment to recommit.
- Catch yourself quickly.

Integrity isn't about never slipping – it's about how fast you course-correct.

Imagine you sign a contract with yourself. It's silent. It's personal. No one else knows it exists. Every time you act in alignment, that contract strengthens. Every time you break your word, it weakens. Eventually, you either live as someone whose word means something – or someone who doubts their own follow-through. And here's the thing: confidence comes from living as someone you trust.

What grows from integrity

When you live with integrity, you grow trust, stability and self-respect. When you live with integrity:

- You don't fear being "found out".
- You don't need constant validation.
- You stop second-guessing yourself, because your actions have already proven who you are.

Integrity gives your confidence weight. Not noise. Not flash. Just truth. It's not loud. It's not glamorous. But it's unshakeable.

Authenticity – confidence without permission

There's a kind of confidence that doesn't need noise. It doesn't need approval or to "win the room". It simply stands in its own truth. Rooted. Calm and clear. That's authenticity.

Authenticity is confidence expressed without disguise. It's one thing to *look* confident. It's another to *live* confidently – as yourself.

Authenticity isn't about being unfiltered or loud. Authenticity doesn't mean blurting out every thought or staying fixed forever. It means congruence – where your actions reflect your true values. When your words match your beliefs. When your outside world reflects your inside world – not a perfect version, but a true one:

- You stop asking: "Who do they want me to be?"
- And start asking: "Who am I – and am I being that person right now?"

When authenticity is missing, you might still *look* successful. You might still achieve. But inside, something feels off. You overthink everything. You filter your words, your energy, your personality – not out of respect, but fear. You're always adjusting. Always anticipating. Always calculating how to be liked. And eventually, you wake up wondering: "Am I being true to myself – or just trying to be accepted?" That's not confidence. That's survival.

Why authenticity builds confidence

Faking it through life drains you and, over time, chips away at your sense of self. When you filter out too much of who you are – for the job, the relationship, the expectations – you start losing your internal alignment. And with it, your self-confidence. But when you show up as yourself … even when it's risky … even when it's not what others expect … you reinforce the deepest kind of belief: "I don't need to change who I am to belong."

How to build authenticity (and keep it)

Authenticity is a decision you make in each moment to lead with your truth, not someone else's script. Try this:

- Notice when you're faking it.
- Pause when you feel yourself "shifting" to match a room.
- Own your difference. What makes you "weird" might be what makes you powerful.
- Speak your truth – even when it shakes.

ARE YOU A SHEEP OR A LION?

A sheep blends in. It waits for direction. It seeks safety in sameness. It lowers its voice. It follows the herd.

But a lion? The lion doesn't blend. It doesn't perform for approval. It moves with purpose. Instinct. Confidence. The lion owns its ground.

You don't need to roar to be a lion. You just need to stop shrinking to fit spaces you've outgrown.

If you never disagree, question or express yourself – you're hiding something. And hiding costs trust.

Wearing a mask

We all wear masks at times, to protect ourselves and fit in. To keep the job, to fit in with the crowd. But masks are heavy. You start to forget where the mask ends and you begin. You begin to question if people like you ... or the version of you they've come to expect. Authenticity is the choice to remove the mask – slowly, courageously – and say: "This is who I really am. This is what I really believe. And I trust that's enough."

What it feels like to be authentic

Liberating. Quietly powerful. Like coming home – to yourself.

- You speak with ease, because you're not rehearsing.
- You make decisions faster, because your values are clear.
- You hold space differently, because you're not chasing approval – you're carrying alignment.
- You become magnetic – not because you're trying to impress, but because you're fully expressed.

What grows from authenticity

When you live from authenticity, you will find a deep-rooted confidence that isn't shaken by outside noise. Because when you're authentic:

- You stop chasing belonging. You create it.
- You stop asking for permission.
- You move in alignment with your values.
- You stop wondering if you're too much or not enough.
- You become you – fully.

That's not ego. That's freedom.

What true authenticity looks like

Authenticity is a full true alignment. When every part of you is working together, there's no friction, no second-guessing, no pretending. You move with clarity and confidence because you are whole.

Full-body alignment means:

- **Your thinking (head)** is aligned with what you are saying (mouth)
  → *You're not holding back your real thoughts or living with unspoken truths.*

- **What you are saying (mouth)** is aligned with what you truly believe (heart)
  → *You're not putting on a front or saying what others want to hear.*

- **What you believe (heart)** is aligned with what you do, what you action and how you behave (hands/feet)
  → *You don't just believe it – you live it, consistently, in your daily actions.*

BE YOURSELF

Authenticity isn't about impressing others – it's about trusting yourself. And every time you live in alignment, you build unshakable confidence. Being yourself is one of the ultimate confidence-builders. Write this down now, as big as you can, filling a page: BE YOURSELF [NAME]. For example: Be Yourself James. Place this where you can see it.

That's authenticity. Not perfection, but consistency. A clean line between head, heart, mouth and actions. And every time those parts match, trust in yourself – and from others – grows stronger.

TRUE AUTHENTICITY

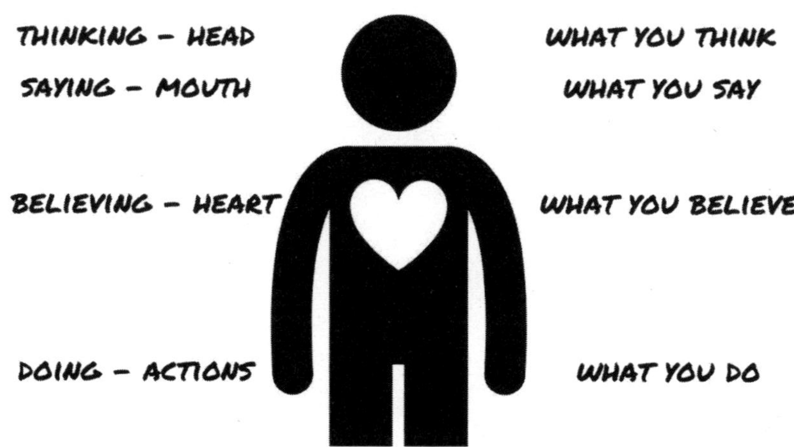

Summary: confidence is the force that builds you

Confidence is not just a feeling – it's a force. It's built through repetition, powered by belief and strengthened every time you run the LOOP – let go, open, own, plant. Its guided and nourished by authenticity.

Let's be clear:

- **Self-belief is a force.** It's the proof that you can hold yourself up – in motion, in pressure, in progress. Every spark of self-belief is confidence.
- **Courage is a force.** It takes belief to be brave. And every act of courage – especially when you're unsure – is confidence in motion.
- **Honesty is a force.** It takes courage to be honest. Facing yourself clearly, without flinching, is confidence aligned.
- **Integrity is a force.** Honesty lived out creates integrity. Keeping promises to yourself – especially when no one is watching – is confidence reinforced.
- **Authenticity is a force.** When integrity becomes second nature, authenticity takes over. Proudly being who you are – without asking for permission – is confidence fully expressed.

Confidence isn't something you chase. It's something you plant, train and build into your system. You don't need to be perfect. You don't need to wait for a green light. You just need to keep looping belief and keep living it out loud. Confidence is not a moment. It's a structure. A rhythm. A force.

There comes a moment when something shifts. You're no longer chasing confidence – you're living it. Your confidence isn't a mask. It's not for show. It's *who you are* – quietly, powerfully, consistently. That's the mark of someone with Infinite Edge.

FORCE 3
INNER FLAME

"Inspiration eats motivation for breakfast."

I remind my clients and their teams of this all the time – because while motivation is useful, it's unreliable. It comes and goes. Inspiration is different. It sustains. It sticks. It carries you through when motivation runs out. And your Inner Flame is where inspiration is born.

Most people think they have a motivation problem. They don't. What they actually have is an *alignment* problem. They've lost touch with:

- What they want ...
- Why they want it ...
- Who they're becoming in the process.

So, what is the Inner Flame? It's not just a metaphor – it's the alignment of three forces that keeps you moving forward when most people stop:

- **Motivation** is the spark. It gets you started. It's the short-term energy that helps you take the first step.
- **Purpose** is the fuel. It's the deeper reason, the wood that keeps the fire burning long after motivation fades.
- **Inspiration** is the oxygen. It's what makes the fire expand. To inspire literally means "to breathe in". Inspiration is what happens when you're deeply connected to something bigger than yourself.

When these three forces align, you don't just have a flicker of energy – you have a fire that sustains you. This is your Inner Flame.

The Japanese have a word for this alignment: Ikigai – the intersection of what you love, what you're good at, what the world needs, and what you can be paid for. This is your "reason for being". People from cultures built on Ikigai aren't just more fulfilled – they live longer. Why? Because they're not chasing dopamine. They're pulled by meaning.

So, ask yourself this:

- When was the last time you felt truly, deeply inspired? Not from a quote or a reel ... but from a revelation. That moment when something inside you whispered: "*This is mine – I was built for this.*"

That was your identity meeting your purpose. That was your Inner Flame being lit. Let's get this FIRE burning brighter than ever before.

Identify your purpose

True, lasting motivation flows from purpose. That's where Ikigai – your "reason for being" – becomes essential. Answer these four questions to find yours:

- What am I good at? What skills do I naturally bring to the table?
- What do I love? What energizes me so much I lose track of time?
- What does the world need? Where can I contribute meaningfully?
- What can I be rewarded for? Where can my efforts create value and impact?

When you write these answers, explore their connections. Create a personal compass. That clarity turns wishful effort into focused, lasting drive.

Living from your Ikigai makes motivation sustainable. It transforms bursts of energy into consistent action – purpose-driven, passion-fuelled and impossible to fake.

Even the biggest organizations understand this. Think of corporate mission statements – they're not just words on a wall, they're designed to ignite purpose in thousands of people. When London hosted the 2012 Olympics, its mission wasn't just about medals. Lord Sebastian Coe, who I later had the privilege of working with when I brought him to our BizX event, set the vision: "*To unite the country behind a team that everyone can believe in.*"

I wasn't working directly with Seb during the Games, but I was fortunate to play a part in the London Olympics – and I saw up close how this sense of shared purpose lifted the nation. It wasn't just about gold medals; it was about *Inspiring a Generation*. That strapline didn't stay on posters; it became a movement. It pulled athletes, organizers and everyday people like me into something bigger than ourselves.

That's exactly what your Ikigai does. It's your personal mission statement. Your Inner Flame. The line that unites *you* behind yourself – and inspires you to keep going long after motivation fades.

Motivation that lasts

Daniel H. Pink, in his book *Drive: The surprising truth about what motivates us*, outlined three essential drivers behind lasting motivation:

- Autonomy – the desire to direct your own life
- Mastery – the desire to get better at what matters
- Purpose – the desire to serve something bigger than yourself

These are internal alignments. And when they click into place, you stop being pushed – you start being pulled. The pull is stronger and steadier, and it doesn't burn out.

Imagine motivation as pushing a boulder uphill – it's effort, strain and resistance. But inspiration? That's like being drawn toward a light on the horizon. That's movement powered by alignment, not pressure.

The spark of Inner Flame

Brendon Burchard explains that the world's highest performers don't wait for perfect mornings or ideal conditions. They don't move when it feels convenient. *They move because they must.* Because their goals are connected to who they are – and who they're becoming.

That's the spark. That's the fire. Not lit for applause or results – but because something deep within you whispers: *This is worth it. This is who I am now.*

This is where your Edge begins. By getting honest about what matters most to you.

Most people chase pleasure. You? You'll chase meaning. Most people set goals to get something. You'll set goals to *become someone* – to make an impact. One path is transactional. The other is transformational.

Inspiration is better than motivation

Let's repeat ... "Inspiration eats motivation for breakfast." Because while motivation is helpful, it's also flaky. It shows up when it wants, disappears without warning and vanishes under pressure. Inspiration is different. It doesn't spike – it sustains. It holds. And it's built on something far more enduring. Motivation is the match. Inspiration is the fire. And once you build the right fire, you never have to wait for motivation again.

Inspiration comes from meaning. It's not just a feeling. It's an identity. The part of you that doesn't just want something ... it believes something. Let's be real: you don't need another fleeting burst of motivation. You need a reason that sticks, especially when things get hard.

FINDING MY INNER FLAME

I knew coaching was my path the moment I lost in the last 16 of the All England Open Badminton Championships – against the World Number One. I remember stepping off court that day knowing I had given absolutely everything I had. Physically, mentally and emotionally. But it wasn't enough.

The gap was too big. It wasn't talent that beat me. It was structure. It was system. It was the weight of a coaching infrastructure that nations like China had spent decades mastering – a conveyor belt of talent, discipline and development. Their athletes weren't just fitter or faster. They were embedded in a coaching philosophy designed to win.

And that moment didn't break me ... it redirected me.

Right then, I made a vow: *If I can't beat them as a player, I'll beat them as a coach. I'll help someone else stand on that Olympic podium.*

That decision became the ignition of my purpose. It lit a fire inside me that still burns today. I went on to coach an athlete to a World Silver and another to an Olympic Bronze. I've had the privilege of coaching multiple athletes into the world's top ten. I studied the systems that beat me and used those insights to build champions. I was honoured to be part of the coaching team that delivered the greatest medal haul Great Britain had ever achieved at an Olympic Games – London 2012.

That loss wasn't the end for me. It was the beginning. The moment I stopped chasing success for myself ... and started building it for others. That's when I discovered my Inner Flame – my motivation and drive for a new path.

From motivation to inspiration

Let me give you some more real-life examples. Take J.K. Rowling – an unemployed single mum on welfare, rejected by publisher after publisher. Motivation might've got her to the typewriter, but it didn't carry her through the storm. That was inspiration. She had a vision of a magical world that simply *had* to exist. And more than that – she believed in her own voice:

> *"It is impossible to live without failing at something ... unless you live so cautiously that you might as well not have lived at all."*

That's not the language of motivation. That's the *grit of purpose.*

Now think about Warren Buffett – the quiet billionaire who built Berkshire Hathaway with no flash, no hype and no viral videos. He didn't need motivation posters or high-stakes drama. What carried him was *clarity.* A deep belief in discipline, long-term value and staying true to what he knew. He's been doing the same thing for over six decades – not because he's driven by outcome, but because he's living in alignment.

The science behind inspiration

Motivation and inspiration may feel similar – but they fire up very different systems in the brain:

- **Motivation** is largely driven by dopamine, the brain's reward chemical. It spikes with anticipation, then crashes when the reward is received. That's why motivation can feel like a sugar rush: energizing

for a moment, then gone. It leaves you craving the next hit – always chasing, never anchored.
- **Inspiration**, on the other hand, activates deeper, more stable pathways tied to meaning, identity and purpose. These involve the prefrontal cortex and limbic system – areas responsible for long-term vision, emotional resilience and behavioural consistency.

When you're inspired, your brain doesn't just feel different – it *functions* differently. You're not just excited. You're aligned. You're not reacting to pressure. You're responding to purpose.

Inspiration creates a neural signature that keeps you focused, grounded and less likely to be thrown off course by distractions or setbacks. It doesn't just light you up – it rewires you for the long game.

Inspiration as a social force

Inspiration spreads. It doesn't just move *you* – it moves *us*.

When you're inspired, there's a glow about you. A kind of internal certainty that others feel, even before you speak. That's the thing about inspiration: it's contagious.

Think of Nelson Mandela. He didn't just speak – he embodied purpose. After 27 years in prison, he chose forgiveness over revenge, vision over bitterness. His fire lit up a nation and then the world.

Or look at Oprah Winfrey – raised in poverty, told she wasn't "fit for television", yet she built a platform that empowered millions through *alignment*. Her story became fuel for others to believe in their own.

That's the difference: Motivation often feels solitary and transactional – "I want this because I need it." Inspiration connects you to something bigger – a community, a cause, a legacy.

Inspiration doesn't just lift your performance. It elevates the people around you. You don't just act inspired. You become a source of it.

Identity and motivation

Inspiration isn't just about emotion. It's about identity. Because when your goals are tied to *who you are*, action becomes automatic. You don't have to fight for motivation when you're *being yourself*.

A person who says "I'm a writer" doesn't need a reminder to write – they write because it's who they are.

Identity follows emotion. You don't just act your way into a new identity – you *feel* your way into it, then decide it's who you are. That's the switch. When your emotions elevate, your decisions change. And those decisions shape everything. As Tony Robbins explains:

"Any time you sincerely want to make a change, the first thing you must do is raise your standards."

Psychologists call this "identity-based motivation". Research shows that people who align their goals to their identity:

- Stick with habits longer
- Recover from setbacks faster
- And act more consistently – because they're not chasing results, they're expressing who they are.

You don't need to force discipline when your actions are a reflection of who you've already decided to be.

Motivation pushes. Inspiration pulls. And identity is what locks it in.

IGNITE YOUR INSPIRATION

If your motivation feels flaky or short-lived right now, you need a deeper fire. Here's how to build one that lasts. Time to grab a journal or notebook.

- Think about your goal. Is it landing a certain job? Stepping into a leadership role? Hitting a performance target? Winning a competition? Or maybe it's finishing a marathon, writing your book or building the business you've been dreaming about.

Now reconnect to the reason behind why you chose this goal. Ask yourself:

- Why does this matter?
- Who does it serve?
- What does my life look like when this becomes real?

THE DENTIST WHO BET ON GROWTH

I once worked with the owner of a dental practice who had a fire in his eyes from the very first meeting. He didn't just want to make a good living – he wanted to build something exceptional.

On paper, the safe path was obvious: keep the practice small, avoid debt, and run it comfortably for decades. That's what most people in his position did. But he had a bigger vision – to grow, to scale and to create one of the leading practices in the country.

The leap he took was bold, even risky. He invested heavily in marketing. He built new systems. He doubled down on strategy and execution at a pace that made others nervous. He was moving so fast that many thought he'd overreached.

But that's the difference between ordinary ambition and extraordinary desire. Ordinary ambition looks for safety. Extraordinary desire embraces risk, but does it with calculation, focus and perseverance.

There were sleepless nights, setbacks and plenty of pressure. Yet he never lost his hunger. Every decision was weighed against the vision. Every risk was a step toward the bigger goal.

Within just a few years, his practice scaled at a pace that shocked his competitors. What looked like recklessness from the outside was revealed as relentless desire paired with smart execution.

The dentist proved something powerful: growth at pace isn't about recklessness. It's about vision, courage and the willingness to take risks most people avoid.

Principle: Desire without risk is daydreaming. But when desire is bold enough to embrace risk – and disciplined enough to execute – it turns vision into reality.

Align your goals with your identity

Don't just set goals to *do* something. Set goals to *become* someone.

Move from:

- "I want to run a marathon" to "I'm the kind of person who trains with discipline."

- "I want to raise money for a charity" to "I'm the kind of person who stands up for causes bigger than myself."
- "I want to hit my sales target" to "I'm the kind of leader who creates opportunities for my family and team."
- "I want to provide for my children" to "I'm the kind of parent who builds a safe, secure life they can thrive in."

That's the fire. When goals shift from *what you do* to *who you are*, they stop being tasks … and start becoming your Inner Flame.

Build mastery through small wins

Progress is fuel. Track it. Celebrate it. Let every small win remind you: *You're becoming the person you said you would be.*

- Can you think of steps you have already taken toward your goal?

Your rituals shape your reality. Build routines that reinforce your purpose and identity – not just your to-do list.

One of my most powerful routines is what I call *"walk and talk"*. At 6:15am, I step outside for an early morning coaching session with someone extraordinary. It's a routine that gets me active, into my flow state as a coach and mentally primed for the day ahead. By the time I'm back, I've already delivered a powerful coaching hour and I arrive home in time to see my family – with the psychological win of having started the day well.

Another non-negotiable is my *8–9am Power Hour*. Every weekday, for well over a decade, I've gathered with coaches to lift our standards to world class – pushing, challenging, teaching, reflecting, collaborating and learning together. It's a rhythm that sharpens me daily, compounds over years and reinforces the identity of excellence.

For clients, it looks different:

- A CEO who built confidence by committing to one face-to-face conversation with a team member every morning.
- An athlete who created a five-minute evening routine of visualizing tomorrow's training – no excuses.
- A parent who used the school run as a chance to affirm three positive things with their kids every single day.

Small routines like these don't just keep you on track. They *become who you are*. Every time you repeat them, you strengthen your identity, build belief and feed your Inner Flame.

Surround yourself with inspiration

Inspiration spreads. Spend time with people who live with clarity, conviction and purpose. This might look like finding a team to train with. A group to perform with. A group of peers who share your career aspirations. It could also look like:

- Joining a mastermind or accountability group that challenges you to grow.
- Volunteering alongside people who serve a cause bigger than themselves.
- Spending time with mentors whose standards and habits you want to absorb.
- Building a circle of friends who celebrate your wins and hold you to your best.
- Even curating your digital diet – following voices online that lift you higher instead of drag you down.

Let their fire light yours.

From survival to significance

Inspiration isn't fixed. It evolves. Most people stay stuck in the same phase – not because they've hit a wall, but because they've hit a ceiling they were meant to break.

Let me introduce you to four phases that mirror the journey from external reaction to internal inspiration – from chasing to choosing. And when you understand them, you stop spinning in circles and start rising with purpose:

Phase 1: Survival
This is the most primal phase. You're not thinking about purpose. You're thinking about getting through the week. The rent is due. The fridge is empty. The pressure is real.

This is what Daniel H. Pink calls *Motivation 1.0* – the biology of survival. It's the original drive to avoid pain and stay alive. Evolution hardwired this into us – fight, flee or freeze. It works, but it wears you down.

In business, survival sounds like:

- "Let's just cover payroll."
- "Say yes to every client."
- "Take the deal, even if it's a bad fit."

But you can't stay here forever. If you don't evolve beyond it, it becomes exhaustion. Burnout. Resentment. Or worse, paralysis.

Phase 2: Stability

Stability is seductive and comfortable. This is where people settle. Where growth pauses. Stability can feel like progress – and to be fair, it is, compared to survival. But if you confuse stability with success, you'll stop reaching.

Now your Inner Flame is steady – contained, consistent, but still cautious. You've built some systems. Paid off the debt. You're no longer waking up in a panic. You finally breathe ... and in that breath comes a dangerous thought: "*Maybe this is enough.*"

You build a neat little fireplace around your flame, but you risk forgetting that even this fire needs fuel.

Routines replace dreams. You convince yourself it's "just being practical." But practicality morphs into passivity. You stop pursuing what you *could* become ... because you're afraid to lose what you've already built.

The comfort zone is born in stability – and held in place by fear.

Brendon Burchard, in *High Performance Habits*, notes that the world's top performers resist settling. They keep stretching. Because they know that comfort kills progress.

At this stage, your motivation subtly shifts, from creation to preservation. You're no longer driven to rise. You're focused on trying not to fall. It's like a thermostat keeping things "just right", instead of a fire building toward something more.

Psychologists call this "loss aversion" – the tendency to fear losing what you've gained more than you desire something new. And that fear can freeze you. Even when something inside whispers that you're built for more.

Phase 3: Success

Success is the goal, right? You've made it! You've got results: Clients. Cash flow. Visibility. Medals. Awards. You're achieving things that once felt out of reach – and you're no longer desperate. You're desirable. Now your Inner Flame roars.

But this is also where the hidden trap lives: complacency. When success becomes familiar, your hunger fades. Psychology backs this up – studies show that success alone doesn't sustain happiness. Thanks to the "hedonic treadmill", your brain quickly adapts to new levels of achievement and returns to baseline. What once thrilled you now feels routine.

Jim Rohn warned us:

"Success without discipline leads to failure."

At this stage, people start skipping the fundamentals. They say, "I know this already," instead of asking, "How do I keep improving?"

The only way forward is to shift your motivation from "external rewards" to "internal reasons". This is the crossroads – where your motivation either matures into inspiration or dissolves into burnout.

It's about remembering why you started. When you shift your focus to who you want to *become*, and how you can *serve*, the Inner Flame deepens. It steadies. And what once fed your ego now fuels your Edge.

Phase 4: Significance

This is where your Inner Flame transforms. You stop chasing outcomes. You start carrying impact. Your life is no longer just productive – it's meaningful. This is the space of inspiration: where everything you've done, and everything you've suffered or experienced, gets repurposed into service. You're no longer asking "What can I get?" but "Who can I help?"

We return to alignment. Alignment shows up when your daily actions reflect your deepest values.

John Kotter, in *Our Iceberg Is Melting*, reminds us that real change happens when we commit to a purpose beyond self-interest.

Hector Garcia and Francesc Miralles, in *Ikigai*, describe this phase as the point where you're living your reason for being – a lifelong fuel that never runs dry.

Significance isn't a destination. It's a journey of continual renewal. It demands humility to keep learning, courage to keep growing and compassion to keep giving. And when you live at this level, motivation stops being a fleeting visitor – it becomes a constant companion.

It's the difference between a flame that sputters and one that burns brightly for a lifetime.

A journey starts in survival and can move to significance when desire meets purpose. Step beyond fear, comfort and ego, and grow into who you're here to become.

Which phase are you in?

Recognizing the current phase you are in is the first step to breaking ceilings and unlocking new levels of motivation. The goal is to evolve, from survival to stability. From success to significance.

Each phase builds on the last. And each demands something new – a sharper mindset, deeper self-awareness and stronger discipline.

- You don't have to stay stuck in survival.
- You don't have to mistake stability for success.
- You don't have to let success turn into stagnation.
- You can choose significance.

You can build a fire that doesn't just warm you … but *guides others*. Because when you do – when you live from that deeper place – your fire stops burning for you. It burns *through* you. Lighting a path. Becoming a force.

The comfort zone

Let's be honest: most people don't fail because they lack talent or opportunity. They fail because they settle into environments that no longer challenge them. The comfort zone becomes a padded cage – soft, familiar and invisible.

It doesn't feel like failure – it feels like ease. And that's the danger – because ease is deceptive. We're taught to crave comfort. To aim for "balance". To build systems and routines that eliminate surprise and uncertainty. And there's nothing wrong with stability – unless you start mistaking it for growth.

The comfort zone isn't a place. It's a mental script. A loop that whispers, "This is good enough. Don't rock the boat. Don't risk discomfort." But here's the truth: fire doesn't grow without heat. And identity doesn't evolve without friction.

The comfort zone is where high-potential people quietly stall. And if you stay there too long, the flame doesn't just dim – it dies out.

THE LOBSTER METAPHOR: GROWTH REQUIRES SHEDDING

Lobsters outgrow their shells – but they can't expand unless they shed the old one. In that vulnerable moment – soft, exposed, defenseless – they risk being devoured. But without that risk, there is no growth.

Humans aren't so different. When we grow, the old version of ourselves starts to feel tight. Constricting. Like a suit two sizes too small. But instead of shedding it, we are often tempted to shrink back into it – we rationalize. We distract. We numb ourselves with busyness, comfort and excuses. We tell ourselves:

- "It's not the right time."
- "I'll go for it when things calm down."
- "What if I fail?"

That's not caution. That's fear dressed as wisdom.

And the only way to grow – to truly evolve – is to lean into that discomfort. To feel the stretch. To shed the shell. Because staying small might feel safe ... But nothing extraordinary ever came from staying in your shell.

WHO MOVED MY CHEESE? – THE MINDSET MODEL

In Spencer Johnson's timeless classic, *Who Moved My Cheese?*, four characters live in a maze. Two of them – Sniff and Scurry – respond quickly to change. The other two – Hem and Haw – resist it.

When the cheese – their comfort, success or reward – disappears, Sniff and Scurry adapt. They head off in search of new cheese. But Hem and Haw? They freeze. They wait. They complain. They blame.

Sound familiar?

Plenty of people stay stuck in stale jobs, unhealthy relationships or outdated habits – not because they don't know better, but because their identity is wrapped up in their current reality. The maze has changed ... but they haven't.

Growth begins the moment you stop waiting for certainty. The moment you stop hoping the cheese will magically return – and start creating your own path instead.

Why your comfort zone feels so safe

We started talking about this in Mind Power (see page 13) – your brain is wired for safety. Its number one job isn't to help you succeed – it's to protect you. It's designed to avoid pain, not pursue greatness. It's why:

- Routine and predictability feel good.
- Uncertainty triggers stress.
- Starting a business feels terrifying.
- Speaking up in meetings creates anxiety.
- Saying "I deserve more than this" feels risky.

Your brain isn't broken – it's doing its job. But the great mistake is letting it lead you. Because the longer you stay in your comfort zone, the more your Inner Flame dims. Not because the fire is gone – but because it's being smothered by routine, silence and unexpressed potential.

When your flame feels dim

Here's the scary part: most people don't realize when they've let their Inner Flame die down. They've reached some version of success. They have the job title. The home. The applause. But they've stopped chasing *meaning*. Their days are full – but not fulfilling. Their calendars are packed – but their hearts feel hollow.

Neuroscience backs this up: novelty and challenge release dopamine – the brain's chemical for motivation and reward. But when you avoid the new and uncomfortable, you deprive your system of that spark. Without it, you don't just feel bored – you feel flat. Empty. Stuck in repeat mode while life quietly passes by. You become a prisoner of sameness while your potential quietly fades.

Your Inner Flame flickers quietly behind the walls of routine. Hidden. Muted. Forgotten. In this space, procrastination takes root. Small daily compromises erode courage.

Jim Rohn warned us:

"Doing less than you are capable of doing erodes the self."

You don't just lose progress – you lose pride. Losing your Inner Flame might not look dramatic. It's:

- Missing the workout or training session
- Postponing the conversation or meeting
- Not sending that application
- Settling into "fine".

And when the flame dims that way, you barely notice, until you no longer recognize the person you've become.

There might be warning signs:

- Maybe you haven't done anything new in 30 days.
- Maybe you catch yourself justifying the status quo more than exploring the next step.
- Maybe you daydream about change more than you act on it.

Reignite your Inner Flame

Escaping your comfort zone doesn't require a dramatic leap. It just takes a deliberate step – one uncomfortable action, one courageous decision. It's creating friction on purpose.

The solution isn't waiting for the perfect time. Mel Robbins calls this the 5 *Second Rule*. No analysis. No negotiation. Just action:

> *"If you have an instinct to act on a goal, you must physically move within five seconds or your brain will kill it."*

That's how you beat your comfort zone. One small act of courage interrupts the script. One micro-action lights the inner fire. Your Inner Flame wasn't built for containment. It was built for combustion. Let it burn.

Find your FIRE

Inner Flame doesn't come earlier in the book because first you need Mind Power – the foundation of everything, the way you control your thoughts. Then you need confidence – belief in yourself, and the ability to keep promises to yourself until that belief turns unshakable.

Only then are you ready for desire. A burning desire. A flame for something great. A future you really, really want. That's the third piece of the jigsaw. Built this way, the fire doesn't flicker – it grows. From within.

Fire needs four elements to burn:

- **Fuel**: the material that keeps it alive
- **Oxygen**: the unseen element that lets it breathe
- **Ignition**: the spark that starts it
- **Space**: the room it needs to expand

Your Inner Flame is no different. It demands the right fuel, the right environment and the right intention. Without these, the flame weakens. With them, it becomes unstoppable.

That's where the FIRE model comes in – a practical framework for igniting and sustaining your desire. Each element is a source of energy, and when they burn together, they don't flicker under pressure – they intensify:

- **F** – Freedom
- **I** – Integrity (morals and values)
- **R** – Responsibility (personal conviction)
- **E** – External influence (money, career, family, recognition)

With FIRE you don't just find motivation ... you build momentum. And momentum makes everything else easier.

F – Freedom

Freedom is the spark of autonomy. It's the ability to say: "This is my life, and I'm choosing how to live it." It's not rebellion – it's responsibility. It's you saying: "I'm going to do it because I want to." This is about finding your reason, vision and purpose.

Jim Rohn said it best:

> *"If you don't design your own life plan, chances are you'll fall into someone else's plan. And guess what they have planned for you? Not much."*

Freedom comes from vision – knowing where you want to go. And from purpose – knowing why that path matters. When those two forces align, you don't need to be pushed into action. You're pulled by something greater.

When you live from this place, life stops feeling like a hustle and starts feeling like a calling. And calls don't need motivation – they create it.

I – Integrity

Integrity is about honesty. An alignment between what you say, what you believe and what you do – especially when no one's watching. It's "I'm going to do it because it's right."

This is where many high performers stumble. They chase results at the cost of their values. They achieve externally but erode internally. But results without integrity are hollow.

When your actions align with your values, you create internal harmony – the kind of peace that breeds persistence. Brendon Burchard calls this "raising necessity". You don't act out of obligation – you act out of integrity.

When you live with integrity, you act because it's the right thing to do. And nothing builds confidence faster than keeping your word to yourself.

Integrity is the invisible current that keeps your Inner Flame bright, steady and trustworthy – to others and, most importantly, to you.

R – Responsibility

The moment you decide to take ownership, everything changes. Responsibility means you stop outsourcing your power. No more waiting for permission from others. No more blaming your schedule, your boss, your past or your personality. You shift from reactive to proactive. From "I have to" to "I choose to."

This is your ignition – your inner fire-starter.

Napoleon Hill talks about the principle of "auto-suggestion" – programming your subconscious through emotionally charged repetition. When you say "I will" with conviction every day, you begin to build neural pathways of trust and belief. You start to believe in your ability to follow through.

Perfection isn't the goal – commitment is. Progress demands consistency, not flawlessness. This is the spark that turns potential energy into momentum – the discipline to light the fire again and again, no matter what.

E – External influence

Let's be honest: external drivers matter. Family, career, money, impact, legacy, recognition, praise – they all influence us. Pretending they don't is delusion. But here's the key: external influence should *follow* internal alignment – not replace it.

When external influence supports something meaningful, it makes the hard work worth it.

Think about London 2012. The mission wasn't just medals – it was "*To inspire a generation.*" That external influence mattered because it rallied a whole nation behind its athletes.

Or look at Usain Bolt. Winning gold wasn't enough. He wanted world records. Why? Because legacy and recognition mattered. The roar of the crowd, the history books, the chance to be remembered forever.

It's the same in business. Maybe you don't enjoy building systems. The spreadsheets, the checklists, the processes – they don't light you up. But you do it anyway. Why? Because it gives you more time with your kids. That's external influence in its purest form – your children motivating you to push through the grind.

So yes – recognition matters. Security matters. Success matters. But they cannot be your sole reason for starting. They are the by-product of deeper motivation – of showing up with purpose, consistency and conviction.

John Maxwell explains:

> *"Success is knowing your purpose in life, growing to your maximum potential, and sowing seeds that benefit others."*

Let external influence inspire you – but never let it own you. You're not chasing applause or bonuses. You're building alignment with your values.

When these four burn together ...
When all four flames of FIRE ignite in unison, something extraordinary happens. You don't just move. You are moved. This is no longer a question of effort. It's a matter of identity:

- Freedom gives you direction.
- Integrity keeps you grounded.
- Responsibility fuels your discipline.
- External influence expands your reach.

Together, they create a sustainable, soul-driven force. A fire that doesn't fade – it forges. This is your Inner Flame.

INNER FLAME

FREEDOM
IM GOING TO DO IT BECAUSE I WANT TO

INTEGRITY
IM GOING TO DO IT BECAUSE IT'S THE RIGHT THING TO DO

RESPONSIBILITY
IM GOING TO DO IT BECAUSE I SAID I WOULD

ENVIRONMENTAL
IM GOING TO DO IT FOR THEM/THAT

LIGHT YOUR FIRE

Freedom. Integrity. Responsibility. Environment. When you act from these drivers, your Inner Flame never runs out – it burns with purpose.

AN INNER FLAME

Napoleon Hill famously said:

"All achievement begins with a burning desire."

But he didn't just mean wanting something. He meant obsessing over it. Visualizing it. Speaking it. Claiming it.

Hill told the story of Edwin C. Barnes, a man who had only one goal: to work with Thomas Edison. Not for him – *with* him. No plan B. No backup. His desire was so intense, so aligned with his identity, that he showed up unqualified, underprepared and completely convinced.

Barnes swept floors. Took menial jobs. Waited for the moment – and seized it. Years later, Edison gave him the opportunity that changed his life. Not because he had experience – but because he had fire.

REFLECTION PROMPT

Ask yourself one simple, powerful question:

- "Which of the FIRE elements is lowest for me, right now?"

That question is a spotlight. It reveals the weakest link in your motivational system. Instead of guessing or pushing blindly, you gain clarity on what needs your attention most. And that clarity becomes the fuel for a reset.

Once you've identified which flame is flickering, go deeper. Use these prompts to bring awareness and activate the right strategies:

- **Focus**: What distractions, doubts or limiting thoughts are pulling you off track? Are you clear on what matters most or are you drowning in noise? How can you simplify or reset your attention?
- **Inspiration**: What or who inspires you right now? Is there a book, person, story or experience you can reconnect with? What could reignite your passion today?

- **Resilience**: When have you pushed through before? What helped you stay strong? What mindset shift or support do you need to keep going?
- **Energy**: Are you mentally, physically and emotionally balanced? Do you need movement, rest or reconnection? What micro-habits will restore you?

These aren't one-off questions. They form the basis of a powerful check-in ritual – a journaling or self-assessment habit that protects your drive from fading under pressure, fatigue or distraction.

When all four flames burn brightly for you, this is what happens: You show up differently. You speak differently. You attract opportunities because your intention is unmistakable. This is where you find your Infinite Edge.

It's the gym owner who opens at 4am every day because he believes in transforming lives. The single parent who builds a business at night because her children's future matters more than her fear. The founder who reinvests profits into her team because she sees the long game, not just the next pay cheque. These people don't wait to feel inspired. They live inspired.

The final shift: why → for whom

Here's the final transformation. Inspiration doesn't stop at personal success. It expands into personal significance. You move from "Why am I doing this?" to "Who am I doing this for?"

This is when purpose becomes Infinite. You become the flame for others. And that is the highest expression of power – not to burn brighter than others, but to light the way.

Because true influence isn't about spotlight or applause. It's about illumination – guiding others from their darkness into possibility. And in that, you don't just find energy:

- You find meaning.
- You find fulfilment.
- You find *you*.

A closing thought: tend your Inner Flame

The journey from motivation to inspiration is the shift from being pushed by urgency to being pulled by purpose. From chasing external validation to living with internal fire.

As you continue through this book – and through life – remember that distinction. Don't settle for sparks that fade. Build a flame that lasts. Tend it. Feed it. Honour it. And let it transform not just your own path, but the paths of everyone lucky enough to walk beside you.

You've built the fire. You've felt it rise. But the true Edge isn't in the lighting. It's in the *lasting.* Because people with Infinite Edge rise again and again.

FORCE 4
REFUSE TO LOSE

"You don't have to love the hard work – you just have to love what it makes you become."

James Vincent

Refusing to lose is about committing before the excuses show up. Most people give up on their goals. Not because they're weak – but because they didn't build this mindset in time. They wanted the result, but they didn't become the person who refuses to lose.

Refuse to Lose sounds similar to desire to win – but it's not. It's very different:

While desire is emotional, refusing to lose is mental.

Refusing to lose is who you are, not just how you feel. Refusing to lose means you're willing to do whatever it takes – no matter how uncomfortable, inconvenient or uncertain the road becomes. Desire wants a result. Refusal *demands* it.

In the last chapter, we lit your Inner Flame – your drive, your inspiration, your deep-down reason to succeed. But now we turn to something even more powerful in the long run: the ability to keep going, even when the flame flickers.

And it's not just theory – here's what it looks like in the real world. Let's pick up where we left off with J.K. Rowling. She was an unemployed single mum, living on welfare, struggling to support her daughter after a painful divorce. Her world was full of rejection, pressure and uncertainty.

And yet – she kept writing. Cafés became her creative cave. And page by page, she built a world that didn't exist yet.

When she finally finished the first Harry Potter manuscript, she sent it off – and was rejected. Not once. But 12 times – 12 versions of "no", "this won't sell" and "not for us".

But she didn't stop. Because somewhere inside her, the vision was stronger than the rejection. Eventually, Bloomsbury, a then small publishing house, said yes. And that "yes" changed history. Today, her books have sold over 500 million copies. They've become a global phenomenon. Movies. Merchandise. Theme parks. Legacy.

And all of it exists because she refused to let the "nos" define her.

J.K. Rowling once said:

> *"Rock bottom became the solid foundation on which I rebuilt my life."*

That's the mindset. That's the message. That's the Edge. That's "Refuse to Lose" in motion.

You might be the next J.K. Rowling in your world, whatever that is. But only if you stay in the fight *long enough* for the magic to show up.

The people who live this way? They're not always the smartest in the room, the flashiest or most talented. But they're still standing when everyone else has quit. They're the ones who dig one more time and find gold. The ones who press forward through fear. The ones who others call "lucky" – but luck had nothing to do with it. It was about refusing to lose.

This chapter is your turning point. It's where mental fortitude begins. It's how you learn to move when life gets messy, uncertain and loud with doubt. Refuse to Lose is a decision, and one you make long before the pressure hits.

So, how do you keep moving forward, long after most people quit? Let me introduce you to the PATH model. It stands for:

- Persistence
- Action
- Thoughts
- Horizon

It's how the best in business, sport and life stay in the game long enough to succeed:

Your PATH from persistence through action and thoughts to your horizon. Refusing to lose becomes who you are.

- It's how you stay focused when your energy dips.
- It's how you stay certain when the world throws chaos.
- It's how you keep going when everyone else has packed up.

And it starts with the one force that underpins them all – persistence.

P = Persistence

Let's start here, with a tribute. Because persistence has already been written about as well as it ever could be by Napoleon Hill in *Think and*

Grow Rich. Every time I read it, I learn something again. And what Hill understood, before almost anyone else, was that persistence is the hidden engine behind belief. He wrote:

> *"Persistence is the sustained effort necessary to induce faith."*

Let that sink in. Persistence builds belief. Not the other way around.

If you've just come from the Inner Flame chapter, you've felt that spark. You've seen what it means to want something bigger than yourself. That desire – that inner heat – is critical. But on its own? It burns out. What keeps it alive is persistence. It's proving to yourself that you won't quit, no matter how tough it gets.

Hill's obsession with persistence came from studying over 500 of the most successful people in the world. And he found that it wasn't intelligence, timing or connections that created success. It was this: relentless forward motion, even when results were invisible. Even when doubt was louder than belief. Even when nobody was watching.

According to Hill, four essential ingredients create persistence:

1. A definite purpose, backed by burning desire
2. A definite plan, expressed in continuous action
3. A mind closed tightly against all negative and discouraging influences
4. A friendly alliance with one or more persons who will encourage you to follow through

You don't "hope" to be persistent. You don't "wish" to be strong. You build it like a system. You lock in purpose, you design a plan, you block out the noise and you stay close to people who keep you accountable.

Hill also described the alternative – what he called "the enemies of persistence". Here they are:

- Lack of a well-defined purpose
- Lack of ambition to aim above mediocrity
- Lack of self-discipline
- Ill health (low energy = low action)
- Poor environment (surrounded by doubters or quitters)
- Procrastination – the silent killer
- Lack of concentration
- Lack of habit formation

Hill wasn't subtle: the opposite of persistence is weakness. Not a personality flaw – but a system flaw. If you're not persistent, it's because your environment, your structure or your internal dialogue isn't supporting it. But the good news is – that can all be fixed.

What Hill also made clear – and what every high performer knows – is that persistence is built like a muscle. You don't become mentally tough by talking about it. You build it through reps:

- You set the goal
- Stick to the plan
- Remove distractions
- Show up
- Recommit
- Again and again

Hill's story of the man who gave up "three feet from gold" is legendary for a reason. That man quit a mining operation just before hitting a gold vein. The person who bought the project carried on digging – and struck gold. Most people quit too soon. Not because it's impossible, but because they lost sight of the vision just before it became reality.

Hill's warning is clear: To succeed, you just need to keep going, just a little bit longer. He also offered a four-step formula for building persistence into your character. Let's look at these again:

1. A definite purpose backed by burning desire
2. A definite plan expressed in continuous action
3. A mind closed to negativity
4. A support crew who energize you

Miss one, and your persistence weakens. Nail all four, and that's your Infinite Edge.

Hill's conclusion?

> *"There is no substitute for persistence. It cannot be supplanted by any other quality."*

Talent alone won't be enough. Brilliance won't carry you over the line. Only the person who refuses to quit succeeds.

MY OWN STORY OF PERSISTENCE

At school, I struggled. Reading, writing, spelling – they all felt like uphill battles. But I didn't know back then that I had dyslexia. I didn't know I was "different". And because I didn't know, I didn't label it. I just accepted it. It was one teacher who called me "thick" – not all of them. But it stuck. I can still hear it. Not as pain, but as fuel. I never let it define me, because purpose got there first.

Even as a kid, I had a reason. I was an ambitious athlete. Then I became an ambitious coach. Now I'm an ambitious global leader in coaching. That purpose – that pull – has always been there. I've seen hundreds of people come and go. Some with more talent. Some with better starts. But they didn't stay in the fight. I did. Because my commitment isn't conditional – it's wired into me.

I didn't have the perfect tools. But I had purpose. And when you're powered by purpose, you don't look for exits – you look for reps. That's why I kept going. That's why I still go. Every day. Through the noise. Through the doubt. Through the dip. Because I Refuse to Lose.

And what I've learned from working with and coaching hundreds of thousands of people – from the underdogs to the elite – is this: your beliefs about persistence shape your ability to stay in the game.

Beliefs of the persistent

What matters most is what you believe to be true about persistence – what it means to you, how you relate to it, and how you respond when things get tough. Because in the hardest moments, your logic doesn't carry you – your beliefs do.

Below are ten beliefs about persistence that I've collected from high performers, in business, sport and life. Read them. Pick the one that resonates most with you. Then build and deepen your thinking and belief system around it.

1. **The strongest mind refuses to lose.**
   It doesn't wait for motivation – it moves through the mess.
2. **Success doesn't show up for the interested – only for the committed.**
   Be better today than you were yesterday. Every day.

3. **The price of success is paid in full, in advance.**
   No discount. No refund. Just discipline.
4. **There is no shortcut. No guarantee. No pat on the back. Just you, doing the work – again.**
   Show up. Shut up. Do it again.
5. **Discomfort is the tuition. Discipline is the qualification.**
   If it feels easy, you're probably not growing.
6. **Making excuses is a habit. So is removing them.**
   One weakens. One strengthens.
7. **Persistence isn't about feeling – it's about finishing.**
   You don't wait to feel ready. You move, and readiness follows.
8. **Every setback strengthens the system – if you let it.**
   Use it. Don't lose to it.
9. **Success comes from doing what most people won't – repeatedly.**
   One rep doesn't change you. A hundred do.
10. **Success favours the one who refuses to leave the fight.**
    That's the Edge. That's the separator.

You're still reading? Good. Because persistence always asks for one more. Here's Belief 11 – the extra mile.

11. **The person who enjoys the walk always goes further than the one who only wants the destination.**
    Fall in love with the process, and you'll never stop growing.

***

Now pause.

Which one speaks to you? Which one would reshape your actions if you actually lived it?

Pick it. Write it down. Say it aloud. Because persistence isn't something you turn on when things get hard – it's something you live by before the pressure shows up.

When persistence becomes part of who you are, quitting stops being an option. What are you left with? … Persistence.

You've built the engine – now it's time to drive.

A = Action

Persistence is the foundation for success, but *action* is the forward motion. It's what turns belief into momentum, and potential into proof. Tim Grover puts it plainly:

> *"Do. The. Work. Every day, something uncomfortable."*

From coaching elite performers and ambitious business owners around the world, I've found three forms of action that matter most. Get these right, and everything else falls into place:

1. **Exercise** – because movement fuels mindset.
2. **Habits** – because repetition rewires reality.
3. **Focused work** – because attention is the rarest currency.

Let's take each of these in turn.

Why exercise matters

You want to lead at a high level? Think clearly under pressure? Build confidence you can count on? Then you need to make physical exercise part of your daily routine. Move. Every day. No excuses.

If you wait until you "feel like it" to exercise, you never will. If you say, "I'll move when I have energy", you're finished. That's not how the body works. You don't get energy and then move. You move … and then energy shows up.

Expend energy, and you get more back. Not just physically, but emotionally, mentally and chemically. It's like a Formula One car. Cold and idle, it doesn't perform. But once it's moving, once the tyres are warm and the engine's firing, it's unstoppable.

You're no different. When you sit still, your mind stiffens. Your thinking dulls. Your energy fades. But when you move – even a little – your body responds with clarity, control and power.

And we've got the science to prove it. The McNair Profile of Mood States showed that exercise consistently reduces anger, anxiety, confusion and depression, and boosts energy, optimism and mental clarity. You don't just feel better when you move. You think better. You decide better. You perform better.

Exercise rewires your brain. It lifts your mood, sharpens focus, reduces stress and builds emotional resilience.

The top 5 per cent of global performers? They're 40 per cent more likely to exercise at least three times per week than the other 95 per cent. Why? Because they're not just training for looks – they're training for health, focus and resilience.

Here's what I advise my clients: Exercise three sessions per week. Minimum. Thirty minutes each time.

If you're out of the habit with exercise, start with walking. Add strength training. It doesn't matter how you begin – what matters is that you *do*.

Humans are wired to seek comfort. Pleasure. Ease. We're drawn to the sofa, the screen, the softness of rest. But that's not where energy comes from. That's where it goes to die. Get up. Move. Expend some energy – and the world will give you more back.

Habits

Habits shape who you are. Habits are the backbone of high performance. Over time, your habits become your identity. We all have good ones and bad ones. The difference? Winners take control of their habits. They design them. Protect them. Upgrade them.

Here are some examples of what performance habits look like:

- After I brush my teeth, I'll write one goal for the day.
- After I make my morning coffee, I'll visualize my ideal outcome.
- After I shut my laptop, I'll send one thank-you message.

This process is known as "habit stacking". This is one of the most powerful ideas James Clear teaches. Take a habit you already do and stack the new habit onto it.

Building positive habits is about becoming someone who refuses to lose. You build ways to reduce resistance and increase reliability. It's no harder to brush your teeth twice a day than it is to express gratitude to your partner twice a day. The structure is the same. The brain wiring is the same. As Jim Rohn said:

> *"Discipline is the bridge between goals and accomplishment."*

THE MIRACLE MORNING

Want to go further? Start your mornings with "The Miracle Morning", Hal Elrod's SAVERS routine – six stacked habits to lock in a winning state before the day starts:

- **Silence** – calm your mind
- **Affirmations** – prime your beliefs
- **Visualization** – rehearse the win
- **Exercise** – activate your state
- **Reading** – grow your knowledge
- **Scribing** – clarify your thoughts

Do that for 30 days, and your identity starts shifting. Not just about what you do, but how you see yourself. You stop reacting to life and start directing it.

Today, before stepping on stage to deliver a keynote, I use the SAVERS principles. Silence to breathe and ground myself. Visualization to see the audience engaged. Affirmations like *"It's not about me. It's all about them. Enjoy."* That one line shifts my state instantly from nerves to service, from pressure to presence.

I use SAVERS as a daily stacking routine in my mornings. Not just for performance moments, but for life. Each practice layers on the next, building a mindset that's calmer, clearer and more prepared before the day even begins.

When you practise it daily – whether in sport, business or life – your identity shifts. It's not just about what you do, it's about who you become. You stop reacting to pressure and start directing it.

So, here's your challenge: choose one habit. Don't overcomplicate it – keep it simple, powerful and repeatable. Maybe it's writing down the single biggest priority for your day before you even open your laptop. Maybe it's affirming "I refuse to lose today" as you walk into a meeting. Maybe it's taking one minute to visualize yourself delivering under pressure – calm, composed and ready. Maybe it's refusing to go home until you've tackled the toughest task – the one most people would put off until tomorrow.

Whatever you choose, stack it on something you already do. Repeat it every day for 30 days. Make it easy to start and impossible to ignore. Because the truth is, you don't build resilience in the big moments – you build it in the daily habits that make you unshakable when the big moments arrive.

The more you repeat a behaviour, the more your brain automates it. That's when it becomes who you are. The science is clear: Habits don't form just because time passes. The "21 days to form a habit" myth? Oversimplified. Research shows it can take anywhere from 18 to 254 days, depending on the habit, the person and the consistency of repetition. What matters isn't time – it's reps.

Every habit runs through what Charles Duhigg calls the "habit loop":

Cue → Routine → Reward

You get triggered by something. You perform the routine. You get the dopamine reward. Repeat that loop, and the brain wires it in.

Focus

In a world addicted to noise, focus isn't just an advantage – it's your Edge. Bill Gates and Warren Buffett, when asked the secret to their monumental success, gave the same one-word answer: *Focus.*

But focus is rare because it's costly. It demands saying no. It demands presence. It demands the discipline to be here, fully – while everything around you screams for attention elsewhere.

Action without focus is chaos. And in today's world, chaos is the default. You don't need more apps. You don't need more ideas. You need more focus. Because success isn't about how much you do – it's about how often you go *deep* on what truly matters. That's where performance is built. That's where belief grows. That's where the real results live.

Focus is what sharpens the other superpowers: It brings clarity to your thoughts. It amplifies your choices. It solidifies your decisions. And when pressure hits – focus is the fuse that helps you Refuse to Lose.

Focused work

Focused work is deliberate, distraction-free time. Cal Newport calls this "deep work" – the superpower of the 21st century. "To learn hard things quickly, you must focus intensely without distraction." In a world full of noise and distraction, real focus isn't just rare – it's part of your Edge.

Chris Bailey refers to it as "hyperfocus" – your brain's most productive mode. One hour of true focus often creates more progress than eight hours of reacting and multitasking. Here's how:

- Single-task everything – one tab, one task, one intention.
- Use deep work windows – 90-minute sprints of deliberate output.
- Design your environment to reduce friction and distraction.

Let's not pretend it's easy. The world is designed to break your focus. And so is your brain. You're wired to seek pleasure and avoid pain. You're biologically drawn to short-term dopamine. That's why deep work can feel hard at first – because it's *meant* to. Though ... that's also why it works.

Deep practice

In *The Talent Code*, Daniel Coyle studied the best athletes, musicians and performers in the world. He found that greatness didn't come from natural talent – it came from what he calls "deep practice". This practice is:

- Focused
- Repetitive
- On the edge of ability
- Full of mistakes, correction and effort.

This is the secret. Growth lives in the struggle – not the ease. Your brain builds performance wiring (myelin) when you're pushing through resistance. Not when you're scrolling. Not when you're dabbling. When you're deep in focused work.

Think of learning to drive. Most people stretch it out over months ... a lesson a week, slow improvement, constant forgetting. But then there's the other way – the crash course. Terrible name. Incredible method. One week. All day. Full focus. And what happens? People pass. Fast.

That's immersion. It's not natural talent alone that unlocks mastery. It's depth and full immersion. Reps that wire in excellence. When all you do is drive, your brain wires in the skills quicker. The world calls it cramming ... but in performance? We call it deliberate immersion. You don't dabble. You dive.

Immersion sharpens attention, speeds up feedback and builds identity faster than anything else. It's how elite athletes train. It's how fluency is developed in languages. It's how breakthroughs are made in business.

"Greatness isn't about speed – it's about deliberate precision, repeated until it becomes instinct."

James Vincent

So, if you're tired of slow progress in your chosen field … immerse. Go deep. Go hard. Go all in – even for a short period. And watch what happens next.

And here's the truth: it's not just driving. This works in any area of life. Business. Sport. Learning a language. Building a skill. Go deep, go all in – even for a short burst – and you'll grow quicker, deeper, faster.

High Payoff Activities

So, where do you direct your focus? What exactly should you immerse yourself in? That's where clarity matters. Not all action is equal. Some tasks move the needle, and others just make noise. To truly win the game – and make your deep work count – you need to know your HPAs: High Payoff Activities. These are:

- Revenue-producing
- Relationship-strengthening
- Reputation-building
- Legacy-creating

For example, if you're a business owner, an HPA might be spending an hour closing sales calls instead of tweaking your website banner. Or investing time training your team instead of clearing your inbox. These activities feel harder, but they're the ones that create real movement.

Then make a second list of all the noise. Admin. Emails. Notifications. Social media. Things that make you feel busy but leave you empty.

Now block out time for your HPAs. This is where your Edge is built. No distractions. No multitasking. One task. One hour. One win.

COMMITMENT IN THE COLD

Winter Saturday mornings in Roundhay Park, Leeds, weren't glamorous. Grey skies. Cold air biting at your lungs. While most people were still curled up in bed, Alistair Brownlee was out running. Lap after lap, steady and relentless, hammering his body into shape while the rest of the world slept in.

I used to coach at the same centre as Alistair, and seeing him on those mornings etched something into my mind: this is what commitment really looks like. Lonely miles in the cold when no one is watching.

The Olympic triathlete's secret wasn't that he enjoyed the pain. It was that he carried something bigger in his mind every time he laced his shoes: Olympic gold. That vision fuelled his legs when they wanted to stop. It pulled him through the pain and made the unbearable sessions bearable.

And that's the difference. Most people give up because they let the discomfort become the focus. Alistair shifted his focus to what he wanted most. The pain became the price, not the problem.

Years later, when he stood on the Olympic podium with a gold medal around his neck, every mile, every swim, every bike ride, was fuelled by that bigger picture.

Principle: Commitment isn't built in the spotlight. It's built in the shadows – in the cold mornings and painful sessions where no one is watching. The edge belongs to those who hold a vision so strong it pulls them through the pain.

And here's where this links directly to Refuse to Lose: when you've identified your true High Payoff Activities, the decision is already made. You know what matters most. That clarity makes it easier to commit, to push through resistance and to say no to distractions. You're not just busy – you're building. Refusing to lose means refusing to let the noise win.

Performance day framework

Planning your week will also help you to focus. This isn't about perfection – it's about intention. Some days will be messy. Some will be mixed. That's okay. Start by assigning a label/theme to each day. Refine as you go. There are three types of days:

- **Power days**: Full focus. Deep execution. HPA delivery.
- **Planning days**: Clear your path. Set the vision. Prep your systems.
- **Personal days**: Recharge. Reconnect. Rebuild your internal strength.

Let your calendar reflect your ambition. Design your month like a high performer. Train your focus like it's your most valuable asset – because it is.

Here's the truth: if you don't plan your performance days, life will plan them for you. Distractions creep in. Noise takes over. Refusing to lose means refusing to drift – and that starts with designing your time with intention.

The 70/20/10 principle

This is the focus formula of successful people: learn from the past, act in the present, plan for the future. Most people get this backward – trapped in yesterday, anxious about tomorrow and completely missing the time that matters most – now. Here's how it looks:

- Spend 70 per cent of your mental energy in the present – execution, action and follow-through
- 20 per cent in the future – vision, planning and strategy
- And just 10 per cent in the past – learning and reflection.

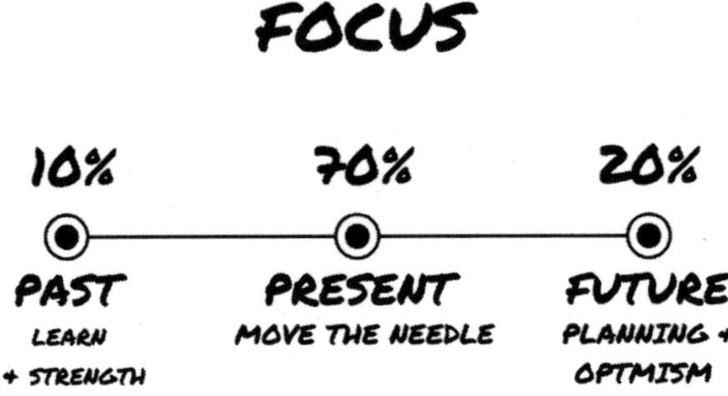

Every time you choose deliberate attention over digital sedation, you become more dangerous – in the best way.

Refusing to lose is about refusing to waste focus and choosing deliberate attention. When you discipline your attention across past, present and future in the right ratio, you stop leaking energy where it doesn't matter – and you put maximum force where it does.

T = Thought

This is where 90 per cent of people lose. Not because of lack of talent, poor planning or bad luck. They lose because they didn't learn how to take control of the one thing that drives every outcome – their thoughts.

Refusing to lose depends on this. You can have the plan, the skill and the desire – but if your thoughts turn negative, hesitant or distracted, your Edge collapses. Master your thoughts and you master the resilience to keep going when others quit.

You've already learned in the *Mind Power* chapter that your subconscious is always listening, always running the code you feed it, especially the thoughts you repeat. Earl Nightingale said it best:

> *"Here is the key to success ... and, the key to failure ... We become what we think about. Let me say that again ... We become what we think about."*

So, the question becomes: What are you repeating? And is it helping you ... or holding you back?

From years of coaching Olympians and elite business owners, and learning it the hard way myself – this truth stands out:

> *"If you only master one thing in your life ... let it be your thoughts. Because once your mind is yours, everything else follows."*

Confidence follows. Focus follows. Action follows. Leadership follows. And with that – refusal follows. Because when your thinking is aligned with your identity, you no longer flirt with quitting ... you wire yourself to persist.

And the good news? Thoughts are trainable like a muscle. With intention and repetition, you can rewire the mental code that runs your life.

Building your resilience

Professor Jim McKenna once told me something that's stayed with me ever since:

> *"Resilience is born at the power of 3:1."*

To Refuse to Lose – to truly power forward – we need to have three positive thoughts for every one negative. That's the ratio required just to stay emotionally optimistic. And if you're naturally pessimistic? It might take 7:1 – seven positive, believable, forward-moving thoughts just to break even. So, the goal here is to train your mind to find at least three empowering thoughts for every one that drags you down – this is the building block of resilience.

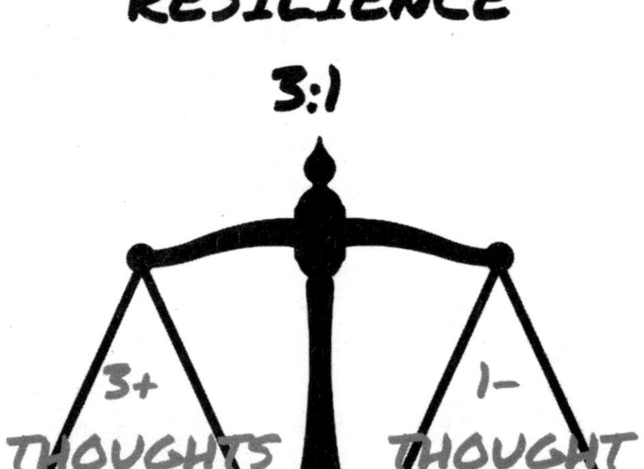

This isn't natural for most of us. This is a skill you need to learn and develop. You don't drift into this mindset – you build it. One thought at a time. And no, you can't fake it. You can't just recite hollow affirmations and hope your brain buys it. A thought must be something you believe, something that moves you forward, something you've rehearsed enough that it becomes real.

So, what happens when you actually take control of your thoughts?

- You become more stable under pressure.
- You bounce back faster.
- You make better decisions.
- You build confidence – not because of results, but because of clarity.
- You stop reacting and start responding.
- You stop spiralling and start choosing.

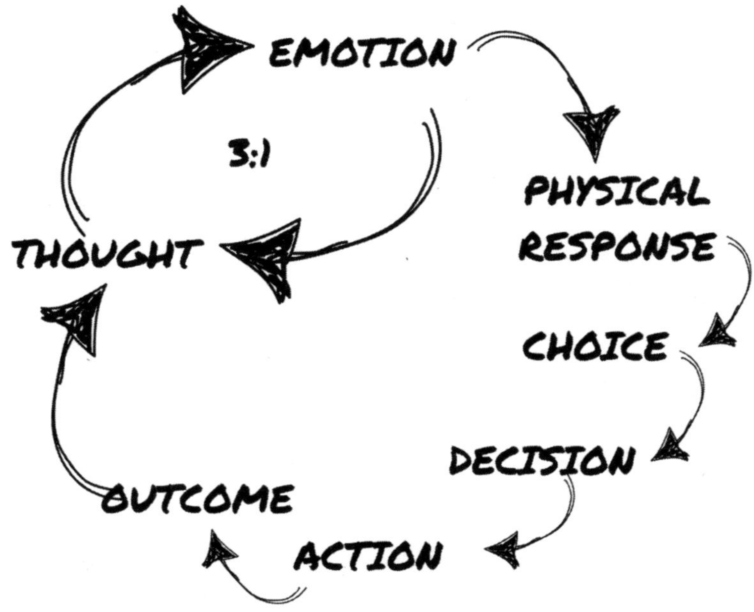

Your state shapes your story. Master this loop – from thought to outcome – and you reclaim control. It all starts with emotion, but it ends in results. Keep the 3:1 balance, and your mindset becomes unshakable.

How to fix procrastination

Indecision drains power. It leaks energy. It keeps you stuck in your head – where doubts multiply and clarity fades.

Making a decision doesn't mean always being right. It means being deliberate. Intentional. Present. Because when you decide, you move. And movement is where confidence lives.

Be serious about making good decisions. Because every great outcome you admire started with one.

Choice unlocks possibility and allows you to explore. And the second you start exploring, anxiety fades. Because anxiety thrives when you feel trapped. But when you have even two options, you're no longer trapped – you're at a fork in the road. That's power. So, start here – every time the pressure hits:

- Ask yourself: What are my two or three options?

Not 10. Not 20. Too many options lead to overwhelm. Just two or three. Enough to see new paths without getting stuck.

Some decisions require speed. Others require space. That's why you must train both – instinct and intellect. When you've got a decision to make, use this process. For each option, jot down the:

1. Key risks
2. Key benefits
3. The next three steps if you chose it
4. The likelihood of success (your gut call)

Then walk away. Come back ten minutes later and let your instincts decide. You've made it objective. You've clarified the landscape. And now, with clarity – you move forward.

This doesn't need to be easy, it just needs to be done. The more you practise making decisions, the faster it flows. Decision-making is a craft – and those with Edge train it daily.

Your four superpowers

These four internal capabilities create mental dominance and identity-level resilience:

- Focus
- Thought
- Choice
- Decision

These are the mental muscles that hold your system together under pressure. Focus filters noise. Thought shapes your internal world. Choice creates space. Decision drives motion. And when the heat rises, these powers are not optional – they're everything. The good news is that these superpowers are not given. They're trained.

Leading your thoughts

So, here's the shift: once you've trained your focus – your ability to be present, deliberate and fully here – your next job is to *lead* your thoughts. Because focus without intention can still spiral. It's not just about being present ... it's about being *powerful* in the present. And that means knowing how to think when it matters most.

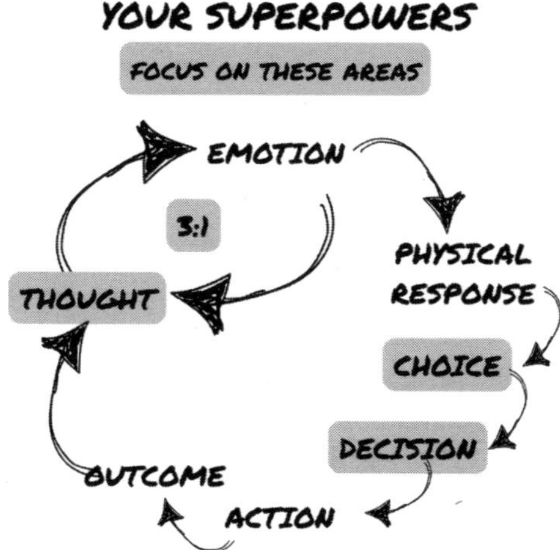

These are your four superpowers: thought, choice, decision and focus. Master these – and you can lead your mind, your actions and your outcomes in any moment.

Why you need a thought plan

The quality of your thoughts controls the quality of your choices. And your choices shape your decisions.

Just like athletes train movement, leaders and high performers must train their thoughts. A thought plan is a written list – or mental script – of the thoughts you want running your system most often.

Your thought plan is your mental nutrition. If you eat junk, your body breaks down. If you repeat garbage, your confidence breaks down. When you feed your mind deliberately – with belief, purpose, courage, vision and action – you start to show up differently. Not because the world changed, but because you did.

Napoleon Hill said it like this in *Think and Grow Rich*:

> "Your dominating thoughts attract, shape and dictate your life."

He also said that every thought, when mixed with belief and emotion, immediately begins translating into physical reality. That's how powerful this is. Start with just three thoughts. Write down:

1. A thought that empowers you emotionally
2. A thought that drives confident action
3. A thought that connects you to purpose

Here's an example of three empowering thoughts:

- "I am calm under pressure, even when the pressure rises."
- "Every challenge is shaping me into the leader I'm becoming."
- "I do the hard things first, because that's what winners do."

You can build from there. Then repeat them: Out loud. In writing. In your head. Before meetings. After mistakes. While you drive. Before you sleep. Repetition builds wiring.

And when the unhelpful thoughts creep in – which they will – don't just try to erase them. Replace them. Say: "Thank you, but I choose a different thought." Then insert one from your plan. When your thoughts are aligned, repeated and rehearsed – the world begins to follow suit.

When pressure rises, when doubts creep in, when the stakes are high and the noise gets loud, don't just react. Return to your plan. When your thoughts are yours – everything else becomes possible. You decide faster. More clearly. More confidently.

Now, even the strongest thoughts need the right direction and purpose. So, let's talk about horizon.

H = Horizon

If you've come this far, it means you've done the hard yards. You've taken control of your thoughts. You've built resilience through the 3:1 loop. And this is where Horizon links directly to the Refuse to Lose framework – because when you have a clear picture of what you're fighting for, it becomes far harder to quit.

Out of all four parts of the PATH model, horizon is the simplest. The lightest. The most energizing. It's the thing you lift your eyes to when you're tired of pushing. And sometimes, that's all you need.

Horizon is the future you've chosen. The vision that lights you up. The picture you carry in your head of a life fully lived, and a version of yourself you're proud to meet one day.

Stephen Covey said it perfectly:

"Begin with the end in mind."

Horizon isn't pressure – it's whispering: "Remember why you started."

Write the answer to this question down in three sentences:

- Why will I keep going?

Make it real. Make it emotional. Don't write what sounds good – write what feels true. This is your reason. Your driver. Your north star. Because this is where most people quit. Not because they couldn't. But because they lost connection to what it was all for.

But you? You're not most. You are not average. You've trained your thoughts. Now you've looked forward, and locked in your horizon. And that makes you powerful. Because now you're moving with direction. With reason. With something in front of you that makes everything behind you make sense.

The world doesn't reward the most talented. It rewards the most persistent – the ones who refused to lose. And the ones who stay persistent are the ones who remember *why*. So turn your horizon into movement. Lock in the process that makes your vision magnetic.

IVVM – the attraction framework

IVVM is a formula for training your subconscious to believe and behave in alignment with your highest vision. It stands for:

- Idealize
- Visualize
- Verbalize
- Materialize.

Refusing to lose isn't just about persistence – it's also about attraction. The strongest winners don't just fight against setbacks, they pull their future toward them. That's why IVVM belongs here – it's the framework that makes refusal practical: a system to keep your vision alive, your belief unshakable and your actions aligned until results arrive.

Before I take you through the IVVM process, I want to honour something important – the roots of this work. Much of what you're about to read is built on a foundation laid nearly a century ago by Napoleon Hill, in *Think and Grow Rich*. Hill spoke of a force called "autosuggestion" –

the idea that we can influence our subconscious mind by what we repeat to ourselves, over and over again, with belief, desire and emotion:

> "Any idea, plan or purpose may be placed in the mind through repetition of thought."

EDGE ACTIVATION

This is your system. Your rhythm. It brings your thoughts, beliefs and actions into harmony – so you live with clarity and confidence.

Read this out loud. Slowly. Then read it again. This is activation. The deeper you take it in, the faster it works:

My mind is powerful. And I can use it to attract the life I want.

Success is something I attract – by becoming the kind of person it naturally moves toward.

I lead myself with clarity, strength and purpose.
I refuse to let go of what matters most to me.
I'm in control. I'm in charge. I make decisions. I take action.
Trust yourself [insert your name].

Modern neuroscience confirms what Hill sensed. Your thoughts do rewire your brain. Your self-talk does alter your identity. And the images, words and feelings you repeat daily become the software of your subconscious. Today, we call it neuroplasticity. We study it under performance psychology, identity theory and emotional regulation. We use it in elite sport, military training, trauma recovery and personal transformation.

Remember IVVM is part Refuse to Lose because this is where goals stop being optional. This is the framework that locks you in – the mental wiring that makes quitting impossible. IVVM takes your vision and turns it into identity, belief and relentless action. It's not just about chasing success – it's about refusing to let go of it until it's yours.

Idealize

This is where you *declare the goal you Refuse to Lose.* Write it down. Make it specific. Make it yours. This is not fantasy. This is focus. This is not a wish. This is a plan. This is not "someday". This is starting now.

> *Every result I want begins with a decision I make in my mind. So I make that decision now.*
>
> *I give myself full permission to want what I truly want. I stop apologizing for my dreams. I own them. I honour them. I define them.*

Ask yourself and write the answers clearly:

- What is the dream I Refuse to Lose?
- Who do I need to become to achieve it?
- What does my best day look and feel like?
- What legacy am I proud to say I've built?

Because every result is created twice. Once in my mind. Once in the world.

Visualize

Once you know what you want, visualize it. See it. Feel it. Live it before it exists. Close your eyes and step into the vision like it's already yours. Rehearse how you move. How you speak. How you feel when it goes right. Use these as prompts:

- What do I feel on my face?
- What am I saying with calm confidence?
- How am I standing?
- What does success feel like as it unfolds?

Immerse yourself in it.

This is not about hope. This is about wiring your mind to expect success. Your brain doesn't know the difference between imagined and real – so give it a picture of power.

1. Visualize before you sleep, to direct your subconscious.
2. Do it again when you wake – to set your tone.
3. Do it again before key moments – to own the outcome in advance.

This is more than preparation. This is creation. You are becoming who you already see.

Verbalize

Your words are not random – they are instructions to your brain. Choose them with precision. The voice in your head is the biggest performance-enhancing drug in the world. Speak to yourself with strength. Speak to yourself with truth:

- I am strong.
- I am composed.
- I am clear in pressure.
- I am the kind of person who follows through.
- I am a winner.

Every word you say is a seed. And what you repeat, you reinforce. So plant the words that will help you grow.

I don't say, "I'm always messing things up." I say, "I've learned. I've adapted. I've levelled up."

I don't say, "I'm not good at that." I say, "That was then. This is now."

Own your self-talk – because it's shaping your self-image. And that image shapes every action you take.

Materialize

This is where belief becomes behaviour. Where internal alignment becomes external results. You do not hesitate. You do not wait for the perfect moment. Move now. Because movement is power, and action attracts everything you want.

> *I persist. I take action. I enjoy the process. I do whatever it takes. I keep promises to myself. I show up.*

This is the moment you become who you've decided to be. Not in theory. In reality.

I do this every day – because repetition is how greatness grows. This isn't just a routine. This is my ritual. This is how you shift from waiting to winning. From hoping to doing. From confusion to clarity. Say to yourself, right now:

USING IVVM WHEN IT COUNTS

Let's put this into practice. I want you to write down three or four things that you want to achieve tomorrow. Don't overthink. Just get clear. For example:

- Finish the project with focus.
- Feel calm and present with the kids.
- Show up as a confident leader.

Now, you need to run IVVM three times:

Before you sleep

Look at tomorrow's goals and follow these steps.

- **Idealize** the best outcome.
- **Visualize** it happening.
- **Verbalize** who you are.
- **Materialize** it through presence and action.

Let your mind rehearse success while you sleep.

Again in the morning

When you wake up, repeat the exact same IVVM cycle. Look at the same goals and follow the same steps. Same vision. Same words. Same energy. This locks your mind in and aligns your actions.

Just before it counts

Right before that key moment – a meeting, a pitch, a decision, a challenge – stop for 60–90 seconds and run IVVM again. This is how you perform and attract what you want.

- Yes I can. Yes I will.
- Every day, I get stronger.
- Every action I take, I gain belief.
- Every time I show up, I expand my Edge.
- I lead myself. I trust myself. I follow through on my promises.

Finding your Edge

This Edge isn't in talent, luck or even a perfect plan. It's in refusing to lose – choosing action again and again, no matter how hard it gets. It's the mindset that says: *I will not quit. I will not drift. I will not stop until the goal is mine.*

IVVM is your daily system for living that refusal. It locks your focus, hardens your resilience and connects you to the vision that keeps you moving forward. When others let go, you hold on. When others slow down, you press on.

This is how serial winners are made. Not because they always win – but because they Refuse to Lose.

FORCE 5
PERFORMANCE EDGE

"Grit gets you started. But skill takes you to world class. Let's sharpen your Edge."

You've learned to harness your mind. You've gained confidence and learned to push through doubt. Now we are going to look at performance – how you make the most of the talents or ideas that you have, along with the indispensable skills you need to thrive and succeed, whatever your field of expertise.

I'm going to share with you the performance skills that multiply everything you've learned so far. Because all the confidence in the world is wasted without competence. This is the Performance Edge. The moment belief becomes behaviour, and behaviour becomes results.

These performance skills can give you a real-world advantage that shapes how you grow, feel and lead. These performance skills build trust. They build belief. And they build your identity – day by day, word by word, choice by choice. Because the world doesn't follow the smartest ... it follows the clearest. The calmest. The ones who've done the work on themselves.

You might be thinking: Isn't performance all about talent? What looks like talent is often just time, effort and focus, hidden behind the myth of genius. Malcolm Gladwell explained in *Outliers* how behind every prodigy is an environment, an opportunity, a cultural legacy – and thousands of hours of deliberate practice.

Hard work beats talent when talent doesn't work hard. But that's not the full truth. The full truth is this: success is built by those who commit to the right skills, in the right way, for the right reason and over time.

The performance skills in this chapter aren't "soft" skills – they're vital life skills. Broad, flexible and scalable. They elevate everything you touch. And they compound across time. We're going to look at:

- Your ability to learn (Kaizen)
- Emotional intelligence (your ability to lead emotion)
- Communication (your ability to create alignment and action)
- Technical excellence

Your ability to learn

Kaizen is a Japanese term meaning "continuous improvement". It's a way of living that says every day, in every area, you can get a little bit better. Small gains compound. Tiny Edges add up. And over time, those who embrace Kaizen are the ones who separate themselves from the rest.

At its core, Kaizen is about mastering the *ability to learn.* Because behind every extraordinary performer is one foundational skill: they know how to learn.

Learning itself is a skill. The best performers in any field – sport, music, business, art – aren't just talented. They're better learners. They've trained their minds to absorb faster, adapt quicker and refine more deeply. They've built habits around growth that make progress inevitable.

The more you train deliberately, the more myelin (see page 18) you create, and the faster, cleaner and more precise your skills become. That's neurology.

But it can feel bumpy at the start. That's why Kaizen frames learning as a journey. Let's look at the three phases of mastering any new skill – whether it's a piece of music, a speech, a dance or a sport.

Let me give you some real-world examples of Kaizen.

Before they became the most famous band in the world, The Beatles weren't extraordinary. They were raw, unpolished and still figuring themselves out. Then came Hamburg. Between 1960 and 1962, they played more than 270 nights in clubs, sometimes eight hours straight. Night after night, set after set, they learned, refined, adapted and sharpened. By the time they returned to England, they weren't just better – they were transformed. It was Kaizen in motion: relentless daily improvement.

Kaizen isn't just a personal practice – it's an organizational superpower. Toyota turned Kaizen into a company-wide culture, where every employee, from factory worker to executive, was encouraged to spot improvements. No change was too small. This mindset transformed Toyota into one of the most efficient and innovative car companies in the world. It wasn't about giant leaps – it was about thousands of micro-adjustments stacking up.

The three phases of mastery

Mastery of a skill doesn't feel like magic. It often feels like failure, especially at the start. That's why understanding the journey of learning matters – because most people quit not from weakness, but from misunderstanding the process. Let's break it down.

Stage one: cognitive phase

This is when the work feels clunky. Your confidence and skills are low. Your brain is working overtime just to survive the task. But this stage isn't a setback – it's the start of your learning.

Stage two: associative phase

You start recognizing patterns and finding a rhythm. Adjustments come faster. The skill starts sticking. This is where identity starts forming – not because of perfection, but because of persistence.

Stage three: autonomous phase

The work becomes instinct. This is what Mihaly Csikszentmihalyi called "flow" – that state where time disappears and performance peaks (see also page 32). You're fully immersed. And yet, even here, the learning continues. You revisit your skills at higher and higher levels. That's why the best never coast. They refine.

How to improve your skills

Coyle. Colvin. Gladwell. Robbins. Canfield. Hill. They all agree that there is no shortcut to gaining skills. There are three ingredients that matter:

1. **Time.** You will need focused, intentional, priority-based time. One hour of deep learning per day, compounded over a year, will transform your skills. For example, a CEO who spends one hour each morning

rehearsing investor presentations will become a dramatically more confident and persuasive speaker within a year. That time compounds into authority, clarity and influence.

2. **Effort.** Show up when you don't feel like it. Do the work when nobody's watching. Repetition doesn't just shape results – it builds belief. For example, a recruiter who runs ten mock interviews a week sharpens their ability to read candidates, ask sharper questions and build rapport. Over months, their "instinct" is really trained effort paying off.
3. **Focus.** If you want to improve your skills, reclaim your attention. Create space. Avoid distractions. Because mastery doesn't live in multitasking – it lives in obsession. For example, an entrepreneur who blocks 90 distraction-free minutes daily to practise strategic thinking – analyzing case studies, writing out scenarios, stress-testing ideas – becomes sharper at making decisions under pressure.

The small wins

This is about the small habits that create performance. The tiny gains. The daily disciplines that seem insignificant in the moment, but when repeated become unstoppable. Whether it's ten extra minutes of reading, one thoughtful reflection per day or an extra rep at the edge of your comfort – it adds up. This is the *Slight Edge*, as Jeff Olson calls it. Because consistency compounds. And Kaizen is that compounding mechanism in motion. This means asking yourself:

- How can I get 1 per cent better?
- How can I make this process 1 per cent easier?
- How can I leverage this decision to get more return?

Deliberate practice

Malcolm Gladwell's *Outliers* popularized a simple but powerful idea:

> *"It takes 10,000 hours of deliberate practice to become world class."*

People remember the 10,000 hours part. But they often miss the second part – the *type* of practice matters. The Beatles didn't just jam. They performed live hundreds of times in Hamburg before they ever broke through. Bill Gates didn't just learn to code – he had rare access to a terminal at age 13, racking up thousands of hours before anyone else. It wasn't luck. It was hours of *deliberate practice*.

Dr Anders Ericsson defined deliberate practice. It means:

- You practise at the edge of your current ability.
- You seek feedback regularly.
- You repeat with intention and correction.

Deliberate practice is emotionally demanding. It stretches your limits. It forces focus. But it also creates myelin, confidence and clarity.

Seek feedback

Average performers avoid feedback. Learners seek it. Why? Because feedback shortens the gap between who you are and who you could be. And this applies in every walk of life. If you write a novel, ask your peers to be brutally honest before you publish. If you cook, get people to taste your creations and tell you the truth. In business, rehearse your pitch and invite trusted colleagues to critique it. If you're preparing for an interview, practise with a friend who won't just flatter you but will challenge you. Even in leadership, ask your team for feedback on how you communicate and follow through. The more you open yourself to constructive critique, the faster you close the gap between your current self and your potential.

Sir John Whitmore, author of *Coaching For Performance*, called it "response-ability" – the ability to respond to feedback, not react to it. The best don't fear critique – they use it. They apply it. They turn it into their Edge.

Emotional intelligence

Welcome to one of the most powerful and life-shaping skills you'll ever build – emotional intelligence (aka EQ). When you master your emotions, you can maximize your impact.

Daniel Goleman, in his landmark book *Emotional Intelligence*, defined EQ as:

> *"The ability to monitor one's own and others' emotions, to discriminate among them, and to use this information to guide one's thinking and actions."*

In short: it's being smart with your emotions, instead of ruled by them. Emotional intelligence isn't a "soft" skill. It's a core skill. A foundational strength that shapes how you think, how you decide, how you lead and how you connect.

In a world increasingly driven by technology, automation and AI, emotional intelligence has become the most human competitive Edge. The future belongs to those who lead with emotional clarity, not just cognitive speed. EQ is what separates the technician from the leader, the communicator from the connector, the competent from the transformational.

THE LAW FIRM THAT CHOSE TO LEAD DIFFERENTLY

I once worked with the owner of a high-level law firm. He wasn't content with playing small. He was ambitious, hungry and willing to be different. He had a big vision: not just to run a successful practice, but to scale it, stand out and lead the industry.

But here's the challenge. In law, everyone has technical expertise. Every competitor can draft contracts, fight cases and quote precedents. If you try to win on knowledge alone, you get stuck in the pack. He knew they needed a different edge.

That's when we focused on emotional intelligence.

We began embedding coaching and communication skills across the firm – empathy, listening and asking better questions. At first it felt unnatural. Lawyers are trained to argue, to win, to always be the cleverest person in the room. But the more they leaned into emotional intelligence, the more powerful they became.

Clients started opening up. Conversations went deeper. Relationships strengthened. They no longer competed just on expertise; they became trusted advisors clients felt understood by. That changed everything.

Inside the firm, the culture transformed too. Staff weren't just working for a paycheck – they felt valued, motivated and part of the vision. Productivity rose, retention improved and momentum built quickly.

The firm scaled – not because they were the smartest in the room, but because they were the most connected.

Principle: Big vision requires more than intelligence. It requires emotional intelligence – the ability to connect, influence and lead people at a deeper level.

Emotional intelligence isn't just one thing. It's a system – a cluster of interdependent capabilities that can be trained. These include:

- **Self-awareness** – knowing what you're feeling and why
- **Self-regulation** – managing emotions before they manage you
- **Empathy** – sensing what others feel without assuming
- **Internal motivation** – staying driven by purpose, growth and meaning rather than external rewards
- **Social skill** – leading with connection, not control.

Bradberry & Greaves' *Emotional Intelligence 2.0* reinforces this structure, with an emphasis on real-world application. Their core message is clear: EQ isn't fixed. It's trainable. For anyone, at any age.

Why Is EQ so important?

Because life isn't lived in logic – it's lived in emotion. And those who navigate their emotional world with clarity and control rise higher, lead stronger and live better.

Goleman's research across 500+ organizations found EQ to be twice as important as IQ or technical skills in determining outstanding performance. In leadership roles, a high EQ is the number one predictor of success.

EQ is what makes your other strengths usable. You can be brilliant – but if you lose your head under pressure, dismiss your team's signals or let emotion drive decision-making, your brilliance won't matter.

Studies show that people with high EQ experience:

- Less stress and burnout
- Better focus and resilience
- Deeper relationships
- Greater influence and income.

This isn't just about the boardroom. Emotional intelligence will give you the Edge in any field you want to pursue.

How do you improve your EQ?

Start with self-awareness. You can't manage what you don't notice. You can't lead what you won't look at. Self-awareness is the foundation of every other emotional skill. Here are some tips you can try today:

- **Label your emotions** in real time. Don't just say "I feel off today." Say: "I feel anxious because I'm unprepared." Language brings clarity.
- **Reflect daily**. Journal what triggered you, how you responded, and what it taught you.
- **Practise mindfulness**. It's not mysticism – it's metacognition. Mindfulness gives you the space between trigger and response, and that space is where power lives.

POWERED BY AI, DRIVEN BY YOU

Throughout history, humans have used tools to extend their Edge – from the wheel to the printing press, from electricity to the internet. Today, those tools include AI. Tomorrow, they'll include something else. The constant isn't the tool – it's you.

Your Infinite Edge comes from what you bring to the table: emotional intelligence, communication, deep focus and technical mastery. The tools amplify it. Whether it's AI now or another breakthrough later, the principle remains: technology multiplies the human who knows how to lead it.

Human + Tools = Infinite Edge

This isn't just personal development. This is human development – a system that adapts, endures and expands with every new age.

Learn self-regulation

This is where emotional intelligence becomes visible. It's your ability to stay composed, intentional and centred when everything around you says react, and you feel under pressure.

Dr Steve Peters' "Chimp Model" is one of the most effective tools here. In *The Chimp Paradox*, Peters explains how your brain contains both a rational "Human" and an emotional "Chimp". The Chimp is fast, impulsive and emotional. The Human is calm, logical and grounded.

"You are not the Chimp," Peters writes. "You are the one trying to manage the Chimp."

To do that:

- Name the Chimp when you feel its presence: "My Chimp is flaring up right now. I feel under threat."

- Pause and breathe, to send a signal of safety to your nervous system. I recommend a trying a 4–4–6 breathing pattern: inhale for 4, hold for 4, exhale for 6.
- Reframe the thought: "What else could be true right now?" "Is this the whole story?"
- Use facts to ground you – remind your brain what's *actually* happening, not what the Chimp is catastrophizing.

Self-regulation is not suppression, its sovereignty. It's the ability to observe your emotion and choose your response.

Embrace the power of acceptance

Emotional control isn't just about managing your reactions – it's about releasing resistance. Acceptance is emotional freedom.

Thich Nhat Hanh, the revered Zen Buddhist monk, said, "Letting go gives us freedom, and freedom is the only condition for happiness." When we resist what is, we suffer. But when we accept it – not condone, not collapse, but accept – we open a path to peace.

Mother Teresa put it simply: "The only pain in life is resisting what is."

I say it like this:

"What you hold onto ... holds onto you."

Let go, and you gain power. Let go, and you regain presence. Acceptance means:

- Acknowledging emotion without judgement
- Not needing to fix the moment – just to be with it
- Trusting that truth is the first step to transformation.

You don't have to *like* every feeling. But when you stop fighting reality, you start flowing with it. That's where real control begins – not through force, but through freedom.

Channel empathy

Empathy isn't softness. It's strategy. You don't need to agree with another person's feelings, but you do need to help them feel understood. That's empathy in action. It means saying, *"I hear you"* even if you see things differently. You can empathize with a colleague's frustration at a deadline without believing the deadline is unfair. You can empathize with a customer's disappointment without agreeing their complaint is fully justified. You can empathize with a teenager's anger without agreeing with their choices.

This matters if you're coaching someone in your team, navigating a tough conversation with a partner or handling conflict at work. Empathy is the ability to listen deeply, sense what's not said and create emotional safety for others to speak their truth.

You build it by:

- Listening more than you speak
- Noticing body language, tone and silence
- Asking better questions: "What's most important to you in this?" "What are you *really* feeling?"

Empathy builds bridges. It melts resistance. It earns trust that can't be bought. In a high-performing team, it's not a bonus – it's a baseline.

Lead with social intelligence

This is where EQ becomes leadership. It's your ability to read the room, communicate with intention and influence with integrity. Do it like this:

- **Train your tone** – 93 per cent of communication is non-verbal. Your energy lands before your words.
- **Create emotional safety** – people perform at their best when they feel safe, seen and supported.
- **Give clean feedback** – specific, kind and timely. Praise publicly. Coach privately. Use "I" statements and future-focus.

Great leaders don't control emotion. They channel it. They don't remove emotion from business – they honour it, shape it and lead through it.

Emotional intelligence is not a milestone. It's a mindset. It's not something you have. It's something you hone. I encourage you to watch people. The calm coach under fire. The thoughtful teammate who hears what's not said. The leader who centres a team just by entering the room. These are real-time EQ case studies. Watch. Learn. Copy. Become.

Because in a world of noise, the emotionally intelligent stand out. They bring the calm. They lead with presence. They change the culture, without saying a word. Let that be you.

Communication

In the game of high performance, communication isn't a nice-to-have – it's a force multiplier. You can have the clearest goals, the sharpest skills and the boldest ambition, but if you can't communicate with clarity, presence and influence, you'll always under-deliver.

Communication is the transmission line between vision and action. And in high-stakes environments – business, leadership, sport or family – the cost of poor communication is colossal. Mistakes multiply. Mistrust creeps in. Momentum stalls. As the authors of *Crucial Conversations* (Patterson, Grenny, McMillan and Switzler) note:

> *"The biggest performance breakdowns don't come from lack of skill – they come from silence, avoidance and fear of difficult dialogue."*

Every performance conversation is a negotiation – of clarity, trust and standards. Words either align or divide. So communication must become a core skill – one you study and practise. One you use to create outcomes and elevate the people around you.

Six rules of how to communicate better

If you want to improve your performance, work on how you communicate with others. Use these rules and you'll speak with greater precision, listen with deeper impact and lead with lasting influence:

1. Have something worth saying

Don't speak to fill silence. Speak to fill a gap – in clarity, direction or conviction. Every word should serve the mission. Before speaking, ask yourself:

> *Is this useful? Is it timely? Is it necessary? What do I really want?*

These questions shift you from reaction to intention – from emotional impulse to strategic influence. Chris Voss calls this "tactical empathy". It's not just about what you say – it's about understanding what the other person needs to hear. Speak less. Mean more.

2. Say it well

The right message, delivered the wrong way, fails. Impact lives in tone, timing and intention. Your delivery determines whether your message lands or sparks defensiveness. If this is something you think you struggle with, Voss suggests using the "late-night FM DJ voice" – calm, low, steady – to trigger trust.

Remember:

- Praise in public, critique in private.
- Don't react, respond.
- Lead with calm, and your message carries further.

Every message is a performance. Deliver it with purpose.

3. Listen with curiosity and presence

Listening is the most undertrained communication skill – and the most powerful. Listen with full presence, with your eyes, ears and heart. Not with your mind busy preparing for what it wants to say next. Voss calls this "calibrated listening" – attention that lowers defences and draws people in.

If you find that people clam up when you talk to them, consider that you might not be creating "emotional safety" for them to speak freely. *Crucial Conversations* explains:

> *"When people move to silence or violence, it's almost always because they don't feel safe."*

So, if you want the truth, you must first create emotional safety. Here are some phrases to help:

- Reaffirm mutual purpose: *"I want the best for both of us."*
- Show respect: *"I value your view and our relationship."*
- Stay curious: *"Tell me more about how you see this."*

Curiosity creates connection. And when someone feels heard, then they become ready to hear you, too.

4. Use emotional precision

Words don't just carry meaning – they carry energy. Loose language inflames. Precision calms and clarifies. So, choose your words carefully. If you have a difficult conversation coming up, prepare. Think about the words you want to use in advance – not as a script, but as a way of ensuring clarity and reducing unnecessary friction.

When you pick words with care, you take the heat out of conflict before it begins.

Second, when you're in the moment and emotions rise, you can use *labelling* – calling out an emotion to reduce its intensity. For example:

> *"It sounds like you're feeling under pressure."*

Naming what you sense helps the other person feel seen. It lowers defensiveness, shows empathy and shifts the conversation from reaction to reflection. This simple technique is powerful in leadership, coaching, parenting – anywhere emotions run high.

HOW TO ENCOURAGE OPEN DIALOGUE

Crucial Conversations provides a framework to stay in dialogue when the stakes are high:

- Share the facts.
- Tell your story.
- Ask for others' paths.
- Talk tentatively.
- Encourage testing.

In business, you might use this step by step in a meeting where emotions are high. But in sport, the same principle plays out in seconds. An athlete in the middle of competition doesn't have time for a five-step checklist, but the coach can embody it instinctively: calmly stating what they see (facts), giving a clear perspective (story), asking the athlete what they're feeling (path), offering it lightly without blame (tentatively), and checking together what might work (testing).

Whether in a boardroom or on the sideline, the goal is the same: stay in dialogue when others want to shut down or blow up.

5. Speed of communication

Most breakdowns don't happen from disagreement – they happen in the gap between assumption and action. As silence grows, so do misunderstandings, mistrust and misalignment.

Fast communication is not about rushed communication. It's clear, calm and consistent. It removes friction and creates flow. That's the rhythm of elite conversation. Say the thing. Say it now. Say it right.

6. Repeat, repeat, repeat

Crucial Conversations reminds us:

> *"People rarely understand something the first time they hear it."*

So say the vision. Say the values. Say the standard. Say them until they're lived, not just memorized. Repetition builds rhythm. Rhythm builds confidence. Confidence builds execution.

COACHING AT THE WORLD'S BIGGEST EMPLOYER

One of the world's largest energy companies with over 300,000 staff, and operations spanning continents. You'd expect a company of that scale to already be decades ahead in leadership and management practice.

But when I was invited to deliver coaching masterclasses to their managers across Europe, what struck me was this: even at the very top, they were hungry to learn.

We introduced frameworks that most companies still hadn't considered – structured coaching conversations, active listening, powerful questioning and shifting from directing people to developing them. We built everything from simple "walk and talk" initiatives that broke down hierarchy to embedded coaching systems that transformed how managers engaged their teams.

The impact was immediate. Productivity went up. Engagement rose. Staff didn't just feel managed – they felt developed. And that difference is enormous. Because when people feel coached, not commanded, they unlock discretionary effort. They go further. They care more.

What impressed me most was how a giant like GE leaned into it. They didn't resist. They embraced. They set the tone that even the biggest organizations must keep evolving.

That's the quiet power of coaching. It isn't just for sport. It's the hidden multiplier inside the world's best businesses.

Principle: The greatest leaders don't just manage tasks. They coach people. And when you scale that mindset, it changes everything.

COMMUNICATION IN LEADERSHIP

If leadership is influence, then communication is your daily Performance Edge. Influence doesn't happen in strategy documents or vision statements – it happens in conversations, in the words you choose, in how you listen and in the signals you send when pressure is high. Every leader communicates, but not every leader *connects*. The difference is whether your words simply fill the air or whether they move people – to think, to act, to believe.

- Speak to elevate, not dominate.
- Listen like it's your superpower.
- Match your words with your actions – because people believe what you do, not what you say.

"The most dangerous negotiation is the one you don't know you're in."
Chris Voss – the FBI's former lead international hostage negotiator

As a leader, you are always in negotiation – not over contracts or money, but over trust, alignment and commitment. Every conversation is an opportunity to influence. Miss the signals and you lose connection. Stay aware and you multiply your impact.

Technical excellence

In a world full of distraction and noise, technical mastery is magnetic. It's not the loudest voice that stands out – it's the most skilled. And skill is not gifted – it's grown.

This part of the chapter is about your technical excellence in your chosen craft. Your Edge in action. Because once your life skills are trained, you arrive at a question few dare to answer:

- What will I commit my life to mastering?

This is the moment mastery begins – with commitment.

But before we dive into drills and frameworks, let's make this real. Because technical excellence is not just about achievement – it's about expression. About pouring your gift into the world while you have the chance. And nobody embodied that more than Patricia Janečková.

PATRICIA JANEČKOVÁ: THE VOICE THAT BECAME ETERNAL

In a world crowded with talent, few individuals stand out as a light of inspiration. Patricia Janečková was one of them. Born in 1998, she discovered her gift early – a voice so pure, it silenced rooms and moved millions. By 12, she was performing on international stages. By 25, she had left a legacy most never touch.

But her story wasn't just about talent. It was about how she used her time.

Diagnosed with cancer at just 23, Patricia didn't retreat. She rose. She performed through treatment. She inspired others. She didn't wait for life to be fair – she poured every ounce of herself into the gift she had. And when asked why, she said:

"I sing not because I have no pain, but because my voice is my gift to the world. And I will give it until the end."

That is technical excellence. A finite life, lived with infinite intention. A skill honed not for applause, but for impact.

Patricia's story isn't just about music. It's about mastery. She didn't wait for permission. She chose her area, lived in it and gave the world her best. Even when her time was limited – she made her *impact* limitless.

And that brings us to you:

- What is the one skill that would, if mastered, change your life forever?

That's the invitation for you. You don't need to master everything. But you do need to commit to *something*. The question is: *what*?

It might be learning a new software that would transform your career. It might be understanding the local property market so you can build financial security. It might be becoming the leader who builds the most successful team in your industry. Whatever it is, the principle is the same: choose it, commit to it and let it shape you.

Let me make this personal. I want to show you how one conversation – one mentor – changed the way I viewed success forever. This story is about my coach, Brad Sugars. And it's about the formula that shaped not just my business, but my identity.

My journey of finding purpose

Brad Sugars is the world's number one business coach. His influence in my life has been life-altering, with his simple success formula:

Be x Do = Have

This is the formula I carry with me every day since I learnt it. It means that to have what you desire, you must do the things required to achieve it.

But here's the deeper truth: to do those things, you must first become the person capable of achieving them. This profound principle is a guiding light for anyone striving to grow, succeed and inspire.

When I began my journey as a coach, I was ambitious, driven and committed to personal growth. I had studied tirelessly, immersed myself into learning, and committed to leading those around me. I was determined to go the extra mile, to prove that success could be earned through focus and hard work.

But as I progressed, something shifted. I began to realize that ambition and effort were not enough on their own. Maturity brought new wisdom, and I started to see the interconnectedness of everything – personal growth, business growth and wealth creation. His teachings helped me understand that these were not separate pursuits; they were deeply connected, each feeding into the other.

Brad's philosophy is genius in its simplicity. He once said to me: "James, your goals have the power to shape the person you become." This truth resonated deeply. To achieve extraordinary goals, I had to grow into an extraordinary person. It was not just about setting big dreams; it was about becoming someone worthy of those dreams.

As I went deeper into his teachings, my own philosophy became clearer. Everything is connected. Who you become shapes what you do, and what you do determines what you have. It is a cycle of growth, success and fulfilment, endlessly refining and strengthening.

Later in life, I added a new dimension to the formula:

Be x Do = Have + Give

While achieving goals and attaining success are fulfilling, I have learned that the greatest joy comes from giving. Sharing your knowledge, wealth and wisdom to uplift others. Giving creates purpose and meaning in everything you accomplish. Brad showed me that life is not just about what you get; it is about what you give back. Giving is the most powerful way to connect with others and leave a legacy that extends far beyond your own lifetime.

One of the most pivotal moments in my coaching journey came when Brad looked me in the eye and said: "James, a bigger goal." I paused and asked, "Why?"

His answer has stayed with me: "So, you can inspire more people, play your part in making the world a better place, and progress in life and career. Your goals have the power to shape the person you become, James. Go bigger; you have got it in you. One of the major reasons for setting goals for your future is what they make of you in achieving them. Take control of the future you deserve. It is bright and it is waiting for you. No matter who you are, where you are, how old you are, or whatever has happened. Go for it and make it happen."

That moment reframed how I viewed my goals. Goals, not just as endpoints to strive toward but as tools to forge my character and expand my impact on the world.

Over the years as my coaching career has progressed, I have learnt that everything is connected. Personal growth feeds into business growth; business growth creates wealth; and wealth allows for giving. Giving, in turn, deepens your personal growth. It is a virtuous cycle where each area supports and amplifies the others.

Going deeper not only strengthens my foundation but makes my philosophy clearer and simpler. When I see the interconnectedness of everything, I unlock a wisdom that empowers me to coach, inspire and lead at the highest levels.

What do you want to achieve?

No matter where you are or what you do, the power to make things happen is within you. Go for it! One choice, one action, one commitment at a time, you can create the life you deserve. Take a moment to journal these prompts:

- What do you want to achieve in life?

- Who do you need to become to achieve it?
- And once you have achieved it, what will you give back to the world?

Identify three skills

So now I pass the question to you: What three skills would change everything if you mastered them? The ones that, if mastered, will multiply everything else. Then train like your future depends on them. Because it does. For me, those three are:

1 **Coaching** – to transform lives through conversation
2. **Public speaking** – to move rooms and shift perspectives
3. **Leadership** – to build movements, not just teams.

That's it. That's my Edge. That's where I'll spend 10,000 hours and beyond.

Yours will be different. But the principle stands:

- Find the few things that matter.
- Go deep.
- Build skills that compound.

Richard Branson didn't build Virgin through spreadsheets – his three skills to master were vision, PR and people.

And Oprah Winfrey? She didn't become one of the most influential women in the world through chance. Her three were:

1. **Storytelling** – drawing truth from others and sharing it with power
2. **Emotional connection** – the ability to make every person feel seen and understood
3. **Influence** – using her platform to shape culture, not just entertain.

Greatness lives in specialization.

Identify. Commit. Obsess.

This is your Edge. High-leverage skill, executed with depth.

If you want to perform at a world-class level:

- Identify your three levers.
- Commit to them as your legacy.
- Obsess over getting 1 per cent better every day.

You don't need to be brilliant at everything. Just exceptional at the right things.

Train like a pro: the technical excellence loop

Here's the loop that separates amateurs from masters in sport, music, business, leadership, art and many other areas that require deep skill:

1. **Learn** – A coder studies a new programming language. A designer studies the principles of typography.
2. **Practise (deliberately, not casually)** – A footballer drills penalties under pressure. A public speaker rehearses on camera and rewatches to refine delivery.
3. **Struggle at the edge** – A guitarist attempts a riff just out of reach. An entrepreneur tackles negotiations that feel slightly uncomfortable but stretch their skill.
4. **Get feedback** – A chef tests dishes with trusted tasters. A leader asks their team for blunt input after a presentation.
5. **Adjust** – They refine based on what worked and what didn't.
6. **Repeat** – Over and over again, compounding improvement.
7. **Master → Then level up again** – Whether it's a Serena Williams perfecting her serve, a Steve Jobs obsessing over design simplicity, or a novelist revising draft after draft – mastery is never the end. It's the beginning of the next level.

Every skill lives on a spiral staircase. There's always another level – another layer of nuance, precision and expression. The best in the world revisit the basics. Over and over. Not because they're stuck, but because they're smart. This loop never ends. And that's the point.

Flow: the peak state of performance

This chapter is about performance – and flow is its highest expression. Because performance isn't just about working hard, it's about working in the zone where everything you've trained for comes alive. When skill meets challenge, and distraction disappears, something magical happens. You first met flow in the Mind Power chapter (see page 32). That sacred zone where your training and your potential lock into place. Here's how to enter it on demand:

- Remove distractions.
- Set one clear goal.
- Work at the edge of your ability.
- Stay present.

Work becomes art. Discipline becomes devotion. Time disappears. Train for flow – and life speeds up.

Skill builds confidence – not the other way around

Every time you show up, even when you don't feel like it, you earn another drop of confidence. And over time? Those drops become oceans. That's where self-trust is forged. That's where performance is built. Confidence comes from evidence.

The closing question: what will you master?

Now, it's time to answer:

- What three skills will you go deep on?
- What will you become world class at – not someday, but by showing up daily?
- What are you willing to commit 10,000 hours to – and turn into a legacy?

Because your Performance Edge is not given, it's earned. Through training, obsession and choice.

> *You don't need to be gifted. You need to be* deliberate.
> *You don't need to be perfect. You need to be* persistent.

So pick your three skills. And get to work. Because brilliance doesn't shout. It compounds. And technical excellence is how you rise.

FORCE 6
ICE-COOL COMPOSURE

"Fire in the belly. Ice in the head."

Bill Beswick, elite football psychologist

You've built skill. Now it's time to lead yourself under pressure like a pro. Most people break or give up under pressure. Now it's time to break away from the pack. Composure isn't a luxury only for monks on mountaintops. It's the signature of all elite performers – those who don't just survive pressure, but convert it into dominance. Whether you need to excel in a corporate boardroom, appear in front of cameras or prepare for an important interview, calmness is the skill that separates the erratic from the extraordinary.

And yet, calmness is the first thing most people lose the moment it matters most. The fire surges in the chest. The noise crescendos in the mind. Thought fogs. Decision turns to reaction. Confidence collapses into chaos. Outcomes slip through the fingers of those who were ready, until the pressure arrived.

This chapter is your antidote to that nervous spiral. Let me introduce you to the CPR Framework – a system forged through performance psychology and elite sport training. It's how those under pressure stay composed when everything's on the line:

- **C is for calmness** – The ability to regulate pressure and access stillness amidst storms.
- **P is for philosophy** – The internal code that anchors your identity and filters your response.

- **R is for repetition** – The rituals that automate composure and make calm your default.

You're not here to escape or avoid pressure – you're here to harness it. Calmness isn't weakness, passivity or retreat. It's the most formidable force in the heat of performance, because calm minds make sharp moves.

As the Dalai Lama teaches in *Illuminating the Path to Enlightenment*:

"True calm is not the absence of noise – it is the presence of strength."

Look at the greats:

- Oprah Winfrey, guiding deeply emotional conversations with grounded presence and calm authority.
- Bill Gates, building one of the most powerful companies in the world – not with noise, but with stillness, focus and unshakable intent.
- Roger Federer, unfazed in a fifth-set tiebreak, composed even at match point.

What sets them apart isn't just their talent – it's their presence. Their ability to stay composed when the pressure peaks. Their mastery of breath, mind and moment.

But here's the truth: Ice-cool Composure isn't just for icons. It's also the secret weapon of thousands of unknown greats:

- The nurse in the emergency room
- The founder pitching with £200 in the bank
- The parent navigating chaos with a calm voice
- The coach, the teacher, the leader who holds their nerve when it matters most.

And it can be yours too.

You don't need fame to master composure. You just need the discipline to train it, the philosophy to guide it and the repetition to make it automatic. The icons show us what's possible. You show it when it counts.

Eckhart Tolle wrote in *The Power of Now*:

"Realize deeply that the present moment is all you ever have."

Performance lives in the now. And calmness is what lets you stay there – undistracted, unfragmented and unflinching.

What happens without composure?

Deals fall through because someone panicked. Athletes make a technical error. Leaders lash out. Speakers freeze. Their knowledge didn't fail them – their emotional state did. The pressure arrived, and their mind wasn't trained to stay cool.

That's why this chapter matters. Because your results are not just a reflection of what you know. They're a reflection of how well you hold your state, when it matters most.

As Napoleon Hill wrote in *Think and Grow Rich*:

> *"You have absolute control only over one thing–your thoughts."*

That's not just a motivational line. It's a strategy. Control your thoughts → control your response → control the outcome. And the CPR Framework gives you that control:

- **Calmness** trains your nervous system to return to the moment, no matter what's swirling
- **Philosophy** gives you a belief system strong enough to withstand chaos
- **Repetition** ensures it's not a one-off. It's who you become.

This is what Thich Nhat Hanh calls "the energy of mindfulness" – not passive, not frozen, but fully present. He writes:

> *"Fear keeps us focused on the past or worried about the future. If we can acknowledge our fear, we can realize that right now, we are okay."*

This is training for now. For control. For performance. So, let's begin – not by escaping the storm, but by learning to stand still inside it.

C is for calmness: mastering the moment

It's time to rethink what pressure is. Pressure isn't your enemy. Pressure is information. It tells you what matters. It signals significance. When the stakes rise, pressure is your body's way of saying: *This counts.* And how you interpret that signal – how you respond in those moments – defines everything. Too little pressure, and you disengage. Too much, and you overload. But in that sweet spot, right at the edge? That's where transformation lives. That's where confidence is built. That's where identity is forged.

This is where the Inverted-U Theory, developed by psychologists Yerkes and Dodson, becomes essential. Imagine a hill. At the base, when pressure is too low, performance is flat. This is where boredom, apathy and distraction take root. But as pressure increases, performance improves – your energy rises, focus sharpens, and the body and mind align. At the top of that curve lies full engagement without chaos. But go too far and the curve collapses, with anxiety, overthinking and paralysis.

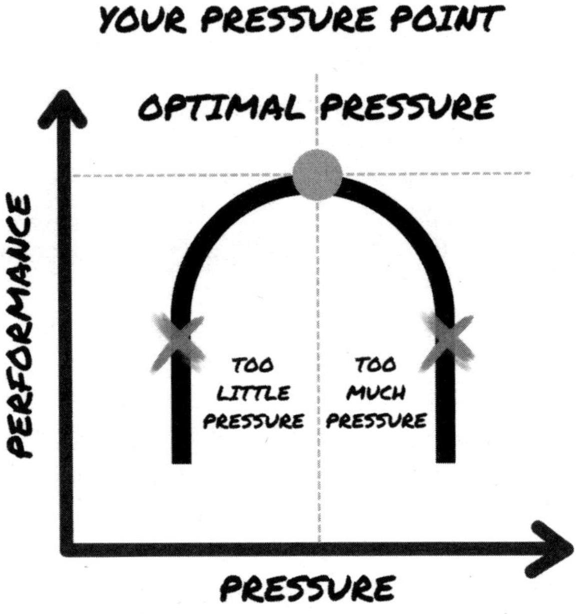

Too little pressure and you coast. Too much and you crack. But at your sweet spot, you perform at your best. Find it, train it and trust it.

- **Too little pressure** = disengagement, drifting and underperformance
- **Too much pressure** = second-guessing, panic and emotional hijack

- **Just enough** = poise, precision and presence

Elite performers don't try to eliminate pressure. They train for it. They learn to dance with it – to regulate it, lean into it and stay at the peak of that curve longer than anyone else. They don't hope for calm – they build it. Because composure isn't passive. It's trained.

The more time you spend at your optimal pressure point – where challenge meets control – the more your system adapts. Your performance improves. Your composure strengthens. And soon, what once felt overwhelming becomes your new baseline. That's growth.

As your performance lifts, so does the level of pressure required to stretch you again. Just like strength training – more capacity, more load, more Edge.

Regulate your internal state

Most people collapse under pressure not because they lack skill, but because they never built their inner leadership. When pressure arrives, they get hijacked – by emotion, by fear, by the story in their head. They default to reaction instead of choosing response. But successful people don't "hope" the pressure passes – they lead themselves through it.

In Performance Edge, we learned that emotional intelligence is not a soft skill – it's a competitive advantage. And at its core lies the ability to regulate your internal state under fire.

- Navy SEALs train using box breathing (in for a count of 4, hold for 4, out 4, hold 4) to stay centred in life-or-death situations.
- Top surgeons rehearse trauma scenarios under fatigue, so that when the real moment comes, their hands stay steady and their minds stay clear.
- Concert pianists practise under simulated performance stress – bright lights, deliberate distractions, even wrong notes played in rehearsal – so they can stay composed on stage.

Their performance isn't magic. It's preparation. Their calm is a system. "Presence" is not a vibe. It's a skill. And like any skill, it gets stronger the more you practise it under pressure. That's what you're building now. You build it through repetition – breathing rituals, visualization drills, thought plans, movement, grounding and pressure simulation.

Training for composure is training to expand that moment of calm presence. To buy yourself time in the moment. To create awareness. To

HOW ARE YOU UNDER PRESSURE?

The diagram opposite shows your situational pressure profile – how well you handle four of the most intense performance states:

- Fatigue
- High stakes
- Resistance
- Critical moments

Take a moment now to reflect on each of these, and think about a time when you felt under pressure. Score yourself 0–10 in each area.

- **0–2** → Pressure owns you. You collapse, avoid or shut down.
- **3–5** → You sometimes hold it together, but inconsistency and emotion often take over.
- **6–8** → You can regulate, adapt and perform in most situations, even when it's uncomfortable.
- **9–10** → You stay calm, deliberate and in control – pressure sharpens your execution instead of breaking it.

Your scores aren't fixed. They're a snapshot – your current baseline. The examples below show what a score 3 (struggling under pressure) and a score 8 (thriving under pressure) might look like. If you're between them, that's your growth zone. The work ahead will help you move every number closer to 10, so when pressure rises, you don't just survive it … you convert it into strength.

1. Fatigue → mental endurance

- **Score 3**: You skip training or lose focus the moment you feel tired. Fatigue equals excuse.
- **Score 8**: You can still think clearly and make strong decisions late in the day, even when running on empty.

2. Resistance → resilience

- **Score 3**: A single "no" or bit of pushback derails your confidence. You avoid conflict.

- **Score 8**: You hold your ground calmly in disagreement, keep the dialogue open and move forward without losing composure.

3. High stakes → risk calculation

- **Score 3**: When the outcome really matters, you freeze, overthink or rush into poor choices.
- **Score 8**: You slow things down, assess logically and make confident decisions that balance boldness with control.

4. Critical moments → deep composure

- **Score 3**: In the decisive seconds, nerves take over – shaky hands, scattered focus, missed execution.
- **Score 8**: You centre yourself with breath and posture, block out distraction and deliver like it's a normal rep.

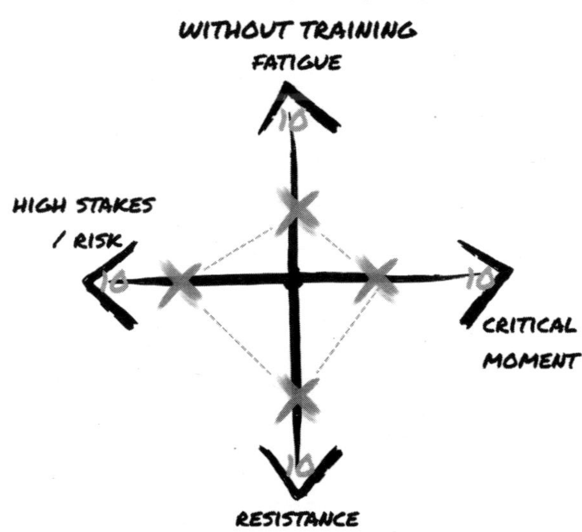

When pressure rises but preparation is low, performance collapses under fatigue, risk, resistance and critical moments.

In this next section, you'll build your competence across all four pressure zones, so when it matters most, you don't just show up – you show strength.

choose better. Because composure only exists in the now. That's why elite performers focus on the present moment. "Now" is where focus lives.

The present is uncomfortable at first – there's no escape, no fantasy, no distraction. But it's also where your power is. And when you train your nervous system to stay there – when you breathe through discomfort, feel fully and still choose wisely – you become unstoppable.

How to improve performance under pressure

Fatigue

When you're tired, pressure feels heavier. Decisions feel slower, and you lose focus on the task ahead. This is why you need to train your mental endurance. Your job here is to build your stamina and strengthen your attention span. Because pressure doesn't care how tired you are – it only responds to how trained you are.

Forget shortcuts. Real energy is built – in your identity, your habits and your mind. You might need to:

- Train deliberately under tired conditions.
- Simulate long days, complex problems and not enough sleep.
- Push beyond comfort – "One more rep. One more minute. Stay in it."

Resistance

This is the pressure of pushback – conflict, rejection, challenge. And when it hits, many fold. Not because they're wrong, but because they're unready.

You need resilience – the inner fight to stand your ground without losing your cool. Here's how to get better at it:

- Practise saying no when it matters.
- Engage in difficult conversations without flinching.
- Defend your standards, not with volume but with presence.

This is where **choice** becomes a superpower. You don't default to people-pleasing or passive retreat when under pressure. You reclaim control – not by overpowering others, but by holding your shape under fire. Resilience is the courage to show your values, your standards, your drive – while staying grounded and calm.

High stakes

When the result really matters, emotions surge. Identity gets wrapped up in the outcome. That's when mistakes happen. But not if you've learned to calculate risk.

This isn't about detachment. It's about disciplined objectivity – the ability to separate emotion from execution. Here's how:

- Break the problem down logically on paper.
- Rehearse the outcome until it feels familiar.
- Use decision frameworks to slow down your mind and speed up your clarity.

When pressure rises, you don't panic. You assess. You plan. You act. You lead with direction, not doubt. And when your decisions are rehearsed, pressure becomes a trigger for clarity – not chaos.

Critical moments

These are the seconds that count. The shot. The pitch. The delivery. The final push. You don't just need calm here – you need deep composure: High-level control. Clean, conscious execution. A cold mind, fully online. Here's how:

- Control your breath (see breathing, above).
- Own your posture. Stand tall, with your shoulders relaxed. For example, sprinters on the start line deliberately roll their shoulders back and expand their chest to tell their nervous system "I am ready." A simple physical reset that signals confidence.
- Use anchoring phrases to centre your mind. For example, leaders often carry a personal phrase like *"Clarity over complexity"* or *"I've prepared for this"* that they repeat silently before high-stakes meetings. It acts as a mental reset button when nerves start to rise.
- Reset your focus deliberately. For example, Formula 1 drivers lowering their gaze to a single marker on the track before a restart – using one fixed point to drown out distraction and reset total concentration.
- Run IVVM: idealize, visualize, verbalize, materialize (see page 113).

These moments are short – but they echo forever.

1. Make your decision.
2. Trust yourself.

DIAMONDS FORM UNDER PRESSURE

High pressure doesn't crush successful people – it forges them. Just like diamonds, their brilliance comes from what they've been through and what they've trained for:

- Mental endurance
- Resilience
- Risk calculation
- Critical moment composure

Every rep under pressure sharpens your Edge. Every presentation makes you sharper. Every challenge is a chance to train. Because pressure doesn't just test you – it transforms you. Highly trained minds handle pressure like diamonds – they don't crack, they crystalize into greatness.

3. Activate your performance system.
4. Deliver, like it's your standard, not your stretch.

You don't rise to critical moments. You return to your level of system. And when you've built that system through reps, preparation and clarity, pressure becomes your platform.

Fear

Fear is not the problem. You're not fighting the pressure. You're fighting the *story you tell yourself about it*. That story shapes your physical response. It either scrambles your system or steadies it.

Thich Nhat Hanh, in *Fear: Essential Wisdom for Getting Through the Storm*, wrote,

> *"Without fear, we are free."*

In Refuse to Lose, we trained resilience – three empowering, believable thoughts for every disempowering one. You don't erase fear. You *replace* it. Not with fantasy, but with rehearsed inner truth.

Presence is a skill

Presence isn't something you have – it's something you build. Over time. Under stress. Through reps. And it's where focus, your first superpower, becomes visible.

Every elite performer trains their presence.

- Lang Lang, world-class concert pianist, uses breath to still his mind and hands.
- High-level speakers rehearse in bright lights and large rooms to make the real moment familiar.
- Astronauts train for spacewalks by practising underwater for hours – rehearsing calm breathing and precise movements in a hostile environment where panic means disaster.

When the world speeds up, the cold mind slows down. When pressure peaks, the composed mind sharpens.

Calmness is clarity – clarity is power

There's a myth that if you're calm, you're not serious. That you lack urgency. That you're underprepared. The truth is the opposite. Calmness says: *I've trained for this. I'm here. I'm ready. I won't be shaken.* So, ask yourself in the chaos:

- Am I reacting or responding?
- Am I flinching or focused?
- Am I chasing control or choosing clarity?

This is what calmness allows: agency. The ability to act with precision, even while pressure screams.

Napoleon Hill, in *Think and Grow Rich*, wrote:

> *"Self-discipline begins with the mastery of your thoughts."*

And calmness? That's thought-mastery in motion. Not emotionless, but emotionally intelligent.

- Calmness is how successful people think.
- Composure is how they move.

- And pressure is how they prove it.

Because in the end, calmness isn't just how you survive the storm. Calmness is your Edge.

- You're not running from pressure. You're ready for it.
- You're not asking for less weight. You're building stronger form.
- You're not avoiding the moment. You're *owning* it.

P is for philosophy: decide how you think

When the pressure hits, you don't rise to your ambition, you fall to your system. And that system is your philosophy. Not your plans. Not your goals. Not your network. Your philosophy is the mental operating system behind it all. It's the set of beliefs that guides how you think, act, decide and respond, especially when it matters most. Your philosophy is:

- How you run your life
- How you lead others
- How you view success
- How you handle adversity
- How you make decisions in the moments that define you.

It's the software behind your actions, the framework under your confidence and the compass beneath your leadership.

As Stephen Covey said:

"We see the world not as it is, but as we are."

That's why this chapter exists – not to tell you what to think, but to help you decide *how* you think. To build the internal system that holds you steady when everything around you shakes. Because without philosophy, you drift. But with it, you lead with purpose.

Don't leave your philosophy to chance

Everyone has a philosophy, but most never chose theirs – they inherited it. Bits from family. Pieces from mentors. Reactions to pain. Half-truths from society. All blended into a belief system you never questioned.

But the best do question it. They don't live by accident. High performers stop and strip it back. They decide what stays and what goes. They choose the principles they want to live by – then train those principles into identity-level habits.

That's what you'll do now. We'll take inspiration from world-class thinkers and leaders. Then you'll shape your own – something that's repeatable, personal and powerful under pressure.

12 iconic leadership philosophies

These aren't just motivational quotes. They're lived systems by some of the world's most successful leaders – each forged under pressure, each a reflection of their Edge. Some are direct quotes, others are distilled philosophies drawn from their writings, speeches and actions.

Read them slowly. Notice the patterns. And ask yourself: *Which of these philosophies could sharpen my Edge? Which could I make my own?*

Integrity and trust

1. Oprah Winfrey

> *"Real integrity is doing the right thing, knowing that nobody's going to know whether you did it or not."*

Oprah Winfrey's leadership Edge is integrity – alignment between who you are on and off the stage. Trust is built when words, values and actions match.

2. Kim Scott

> From *Radical Candor*: *"Care personally, challenge directly."*

Kim Scott's philosophy is: kindness is clarity. Leaders grow people when they speak the truth with genuine care.

People and culture

3. Richard Branson

> *"Take care of your employees, and they'll take care of your business."*

Branson shows that culture and people aren't fluff – they are the foundation of performance.

4. Barack Obama

From his 2004 DNC speech: *"If you're walking down the right path and you're willing to keep walking, eventually you'll make progress."*

Obama's Edge was belief in people, elevating discourse and modelling composure under pressure.

Resilience and service

5. Winston Churchill

> *"Success is not final, failure is not fatal: it is the courage to continue that counts."*

Churchill embodied steadiness when the world wobbled.

6. Nelson Mandela

From *Long Walk to Freedom*: forgiveness and unity were more powerful than ego or revenge. His leadership Edge was service, not self.

Mindset and belief

7. Rhonda Byrne

From *The Secret*: belief shapes reality. What you think and feel creates what you experience.

8. Brené Brown

From *Daring Greatly*: *"Vulnerability is not weakness; it's our greatest measure of courage."*

Brown's research shows that innovation, trust and connection begin with honesty and openness.

Action and innovation

9. Mel Robbins

From *The 5 Second Rule*: *"You are never going to feel like it. You have to parent yourself. You have to force yourself."*

Robbins' philosophy is a system to disrupt hesitation and build bold action.

11. JIM ROHN – THE ANT PHILOSOPHY

When I talk to leaders about philosophy, I often start with something deceptively simple: Jim Rohn's *Ant Philosophy*.

I use it with clients regularly, because it strips away all the noise and shows the raw power of having a philosophy you can actually live by. I'll often play them Rohn speaking about it – his calm, simple delivery lands hard. It makes people stop and think. And then I ask: *"That's the ant's philosophy ... what's yours?"*

Because here's the truth: even the smallest creature has a philosophy. Ants are not strong alone, but they are unstoppable together because of how they think and act. They prove that clarity of philosophy – no matter how small or simple – builds resilience under pressure.

This is why the Ant Philosophy resonates so deeply. It's about resilience, belief and consistency. It's repeatable, sharp and universal.

- Ants never quit – if blocked, they find another way.
- Ants think about winter in summer – always prepare.
- Ants think about summer in winter – always believe.
- Ants gather all they can – full effort, no excuses.

If something as small as an ant can live by a philosophy ...
why wouldn't you?

10. Elon Musk
From a SpaceX interview: *"Failure is an option here. If things are not failing, you are not innovating enough."*

Musk's Edge: Think big, act fast and obsess about the future.

These philosophies are working systems. Together they prove: when clarity of philosophy sharpens, clarity of action follows. Here are two more to inspire you:

12. Don Miguel Ruiz
A complete code for personal clarity, the four disciplines of Don Miguel Ruiz help you stay grounded when life gets noisy:

- **Be impeccable with your word** – Speak with integrity. Say what you mean. Avoid gossip and complaints – precision creates power.
- **Don't take anything personally** – People's actions reflect them, not you. Detachment is maturity.
- **Don't make assumptions** – Clarity beats fiction. Ask. Confirm. Understand.
- **Always do your best** – Your best will vary, but showing up fully – always – builds confidence without regret.

The MBT framework

Many leaders have used this next model to shape their personal philosophy. It's simple, but it works. I first heard it from Mark Bawden, the world's number one body language expert. He told me: "This is how leaders become more followable."

- **M – Make a choice**
  Decide what you stand for. Clearly. Publicly. Boldly. A vague leader is forgettable. A committed one is followable. Emotional intelligence, for example, might be your core: "I choose to stay calm, respond wisely and lead with awareness." That becomes your anchor.

- **B – Go bigger**
  Scale that choice. Build your vision around it. Make it clear to others. Repeat it until it becomes part of your identity. Express it through your actions and voice. Leaders don't whisper their standards.

- **T – Keep it tidy**
  Stick to your choice. Don't bolt on ten new ideas every week. Stay true. Be consistent. Let people trust what you bring. Communicate it relentlessly. That's how brands – and leaders – become recognizable and trusted.

That's how you build a philosophy that others can see, feel and follow. One coach I worked with chose "emotional intelligence" as their leadership cornerstone. Their choice? Emotional Intelligence. Their MBT?

M – Lead with EQ.
B – Build fluency across the team.

T – Make it visible in every moment, message and meeting.

That became their leadership signature. Their culture. Their Edge.

Design a philosophy you can live by

You've seen how the world's best do it. Now it's time to shape your own philosophy. This part is simple, but not easy. It's reflective work. Because a great philosophy isn't a quote you pin to your wall – it's a decision you live by when the pressure hits. Your philosophy becomes your anchor under stress. So, here's how to build it:

Take a moment with each of the following five questions. Go deep. Be honest. I include an example from one of my coaching clients to guide you.

1. **What's the non-negotiable truth you live by – even under pressure?**
   This is your bedrock. The belief that doesn't break, even when it's inconvenient.

   Sam's answer: "Character is everything. I'd rather lose doing the right thing than win by compromise."

2. **What thought gives you strength when things go wrong?**
   This is your stabilizer. The sentence that brings you back to centre when everything feels like it's falling apart.

   Sam's answer: "Every problem is a test of who I'm becoming. I've handled worse. I'll handle this."

3. **What do you believe that makes your vision feel possible and worth fighting for?**
   This is your inner fire. It's the belief that turns effort into purpose, and pain into persistence.

   Sam's answer: "The future I want already exists – I just have to step into it. Bit by bit. Boldly."

4. **Who sharpens you, and what does that say about who you need on your journey?**
   Your close circle shapes your standard. Identify who makes you better ... and why.

Sam's answer: "My coach challenges my blind spots. My wife grounds me. My team expects my best. I need truth-tellers, not cheerleaders."

5. **What belief of yours – if shared – could make others stronger?** This is your leadership gift. The part of your code that others can live better by.

   Sam's answer: "Success should multiply good. Build something great ... and use it to lift others."

Lock it in: philosophy in action

You've now built something most people never do – a clear, personal philosophy. Not borrowed or inherited. Chosen. Because this is the code you'll live by when the stakes rise. It's how you stay you – under pressure, in the spotlight and through uncertainty. Whether it's one sentence or a guiding system, your philosophy becomes the glue between who you are and how you lead.

And here's the truth: **If you don't live by your philosophy, you'll live by someone else's.**

So, stay close to it. Speak it out loud. Refine it often. Let it be the system that strengthens you when motivation fades. And remember – philosophy is the bridge between thought and behaviour. It's how belief becomes action. And how action becomes identity.

R is for repetition: the secret to consistency

You've built your Edge. Now you make it permanent. Throughout this book, you've trained your mind, shaped your thoughts, made powerful choices and built a belief system that refuses to quit. You've developed clarity, control and composure under pressure. But there's one more step – the step that makes all of it last: repetition.

It's not flashy. It doesn't go viral. But it's the difference between a spark and a fire that never goes out. Repetition is what makes every other force stick. Repetition builds rhythm. Rhythm creates confidence. Confidence delivers results. While the world sees the highlight reel, what lies beneath is a grind few are willing to endure.

James Clear, in *Atomic Habits*, offers a powerful truth:

> *"You do not rise to the level of your goals. You fall to the level of your systems."*

Repetition is your system. It sculpts effort into reliable performance. It is the quiet, unsexy work that builds championship and performance habits.

The greats are not obsessed with outcomes – they are obsessed with repetitions. Repetition is how they rehearse success before the world sees it. Johnny Wilkinson, one of rugby's all-time stars, was often seen on the pitch *after* training had ended, practising kicks on his own. While others were cooling down, he was locking in his routine. Over and over. Because when the pressure comes – only the trained respond.

Seth Godin, one of the most prolific marketers in the world, has written a blog post every single day – for over 8,000 days. He doesn't wait for inspiration. He trains it. His creativity is consistent because his discipline is. This is the real separator. Repetition is the difference between being *interested* and being *committed.*

Repetition builds reputation

Repetition doesn't just build habits – it builds identity. And identity becomes the compass that guides your choices, especially under pressure. The more you repeat a behaviour, the more it stops being something you do, and starts becoming who you are. Reputation is the public echo of private discipline.

Do something consistently and you begin to see yourself differently. Train or rehearse daily and you stop needing motivation to get started. Follow through when it's hard and you start believing you're the kind of person who does what needs to be done, regardless of mood. That belief shapes your behaviour. And over time, your behaviour shapes your results.

This is the foundation of high performance. If you see yourself as someone who follows through, who respects the process, who keeps promises to themselves – then consistency becomes part of your character. Not just a tool you use, but a truth you live.

As Don Miguel Ruiz reminds us in *The Four Agreements*:

> *"Always do your best – especially when no one is watching."*

The elite understand this. They don't chase motivation – they build rituals. They know that when a behaviour becomes ritualized, it bypasses resistance. It no longer requires a decision. It simply runs, like a background process. Amateurs wait to feel good. Pros do it until it feels natural.

Repetition isn't about perfection. It's about persistence. You don't have to get it right every time. You just have to keep showing up – relentlessly, repeatedly, until it becomes who you are.

Repetition can be boring (and that's the point)

Here's the hard truth that few are willing to say out loud: mastery can be boring. Not all the time – but often enough to test you. The path to distinction isn't marked by fireworks or fanfare. It's marked by quiet repetition, sustained effort and deliberate focus – long after the applause fades and the novelty wears off.

Boredom is the test. And it's not just any test – it's the filter. It separates the curious from the committed. Mastery belongs to the one who keeps showing up when it's tedious, thankless and unseen.

- **Writers like Stephen King** commit to writing 1,000 words every single day – even when the words come slowly, even when inspiration is absent.
- **Surgeons** rehearse the same procedures over and over in simulation before they ever operate on a human being. Lives depend on repetition.
- **Entrepreneurs** make the same pitches, refine the same decks, have the same conversations hundreds of times before one breakthrough "yes" shifts everything.

That's the point. Mastery is not built in highlight reels. It's built in the unseen hours and the courage to keep showing up when excitement fades. That's what repetition is. Not mindless grind – but targeted effort, applied daily, in the direction of growth.

The greats aren't immune to boredom. They've just made peace with it. Not because they love the monotony, but because they understand what lives on the other side of it: reliability, resilience and rhythm.

As Stephen Covey reminds us:

"The key is not to prioritize what's on your schedule, but to schedule your priorities."

And when you schedule repetition – when you ritualize your most important behaviours – you remove willpower from the equation. You stop relying on mood. You start operating on mission. That's when success stops being a surprise, and starts becoming inevitable.

Training calmness through repetition

Repetition doesn't just build skill – it builds calm. The kind of calm that holds steady when pressure spikes. The kind of calm that doesn't flinch when the world shakes. Because calmness under pressure isn't a gift some people are born with – it's a trained response. A nervous system that's been rehearsed to choose control instead of chaos.

Paramedics don't wait to find out how they'll respond when a life is on the line. They train it. Over and over again, they simulate trauma scenarios – cardiac arrests, car crashes, crises in motion – until the response becomes automatic: steady breath, clear thinking and decisive action.

Dentists rehearse every movement until their hands operate with precision. Their confidence is earned through hours of deliberate repetition, crafting muscle memory and mental clarity.

Speakers who command the stage, know the power of rehearsal. They practise until their message flows effortlessly – not just in words, but in presence. Under scrutiny, they don't shrink – they rise. Not because they're fearless, but because they've trained their mind to stay present when most people want to run.

Why does it work? Because repetition rewires your system. It replaces panic with presence. Doubt with discipline. It turns reactivity into readiness. And in the heat of the moment, what you've repeated is what you'll rely on.

Repetition isn't just how you perform. It's how you stay calm enough to perform when it counts.

Repetition is growth, not grind

The myth of sudden success is seductive. It whispers of shortcuts. It glamorizes luck. But the truth is far more powerful – and far more reliable: you become what you repeat.

Yes, repetition can feel like a grind. Every push-up. Every journal entry. Every cold call. Every quiet rehearsal behind closed doors. It's not always glamorous. It's not always loud. But reframed, it's something far more powerful: a form of meditation. Every rep is a declaration. Every session is a vote. You're not just doing the thing – you're becoming the kind of person who does the thing. Repetition is identity in motion.

Because mastery isn't built in a moment – it's assembled over time, in silence, through consistency.

And here's the liberating truth: you don't need to be extreme. You just need to be consistent. You don't need ten perfect reps. You need one honest rep – repeated. With presence. With purpose. With pride. That's how growth compounds.

Final word: cold mind – hot results

The world loves fire. Explosive ambition. Blazing passion. Fierce energy. Power. Drive.

We celebrate those who burn bright. But look more closely at those who last – the serial winners, the legacy builders, the quiet dominators – and you'll find something else entirely.

They burn inside, but they don't burn out. They hold their position with discipline. With direction. With control. They move through chaos not with panic, but with poise. They lead not with noise, but with precision. They have cold minds.

Because in the storm of competition, passion alone will melt you. Emotion untamed will exhaust you. The ones who survive – and win – are the ones who stay cool when everything around them gets hot. The cold mind is not passive. It's not robotic. It's the ultimate weapon: calculated, steady and surgical. The cold mind delivers hot results.

The cold mind returns you to now. It pulls your awareness out of worry and back into wisdom. It strips away noise and restores signal. It stops you flinching and helps you focus. In that focus lies power.

Legacy is not built in the spotlight. It's not the fiery speech or the viral success that defines you. Legacy is built on a Monday morning when no one is watching. When it's raining. When you're tired. When it would be easier to scroll, snooze or step back – but you step in.

The best don't train for applause. They train because it's who they are. They don't just practise when it's convenient. They practise because it's consistent. And that consistency becomes their Edge.

Most people either burn too hot – reacting, rushing, overreaching – or freeze completely, paralyzed by pressure.

Those with Infinite Edge balance both. They carry fire in the belly – the relentless desire to grow, win and serve something bigger than themselves. And they cultivate ice in the head – clarity, poise, control.

And you've trained for this, through the CPR Framework:

- Calmness gives you clarity under chaos.
- Philosophy gives you direction when doubt creeps in.
- Repetition gives you durability when others fade.

Because the world doesn't need more drama. It needs more discipline. It doesn't need more flashes. It needs more follow-through. Train your cold mind. Deliver hot results. Every. Single. Time.

INFINITE EDGE

"What happens when every force aligns? One identity. One system. One Infinite Edge."

You started this book as a seeker – searching for more clarity, more power, more consistency. You finish it as something more. Someone who doesn't just hope to succeed ... but knows *how* to. This isn't the end of your journey – this is the start of finding your Infinite Edge.

You've built your foundation. You've trained your forces. You've done the work most never commit to. You've looked inward, challenged your thinking, upgraded your mindset and turned principles into power. Each page has taken you deeper – not into information, but into identity. Because winning isn't about knowing more. It's about *becoming* more.

In this chapter, we look at where that shift becomes real. This is where the work you've done so far turns into the life you want to lead.

The six Inner Forces united

You're not the same person who opened this book. Why? Because you've activated six Inner Forces most people go their whole life without training. All these forces now live in you:

- You've built your **Mind Power** – learning to programme your thoughts, override limits, and lead your inner world like a master.
- You've strengthened your **Confidence LOOP** – no longer waiting to feel ready, but looping belief into being and building identity from the inside out.
- You've ignited your **Inner Flame** – fuelling your days with purpose, not pressure. Your actions are no longer driven by fear, but by fire.

- You've embodied the force of **Refuse to Lose** – quitting is no longer an option, because it's no longer who you are.
- You've sharpened your **Performance Edge** – not through talent alone, but through training. You've chosen mastery, embraced deliberate development and committed to compounding your skill.
- And you've cultivated **Ice-cool Composure** – so when the pressure rises, you don't panic. You stay grounded, present and in control.

You've become someone different. Someone focused. Someone fierce. Someone with impact. And this is just the beginning for you.

But before you close this book, let me offer one final story:

I was sitting with my journal, thinking about the journey so far. From that kid who dreamed of Olympic medals ... to the coach guiding others toward them. From the young leader stumbling through his first talks ... to a voice heard on global stages. And in that moment – pen in hand, silence around me – something shifted. I saw it all, not as a list of achievements, but as proof that the forces I've written about in this book are real. Not theory. Not philosophy. Lived.

Each of the six Inner Forces has shaped me – and I hope they've now shaped you too.

Mind Power taught me this: You don't rise from wishing – you rise from wiring. The moment you take control of your thoughts, the world stops controlling you.

Confidence LOOP taught me this: Confidence isn't loud. It's not show. It's not ego. It's a quiet loop you run in private. Confidence is built, one promise kept at a time.

Inner Flame taught me this: Purpose is fierce. It's what drags you out of darkness, what sharpens your decisions, what fuels your stretch. It's not what you do – it's why you refuse to stop doing it.

Refuse to Lose taught me this: Persistence is a decision. And identity beats motivation, every time.

Performance Edge taught me this: Talent is a nice start. But mastery is earned. Every day, every rep, every drop of feedback.

Ice-cool Composure taught me this: The world will test you. Life will throw fire at your feet. But when you train your nervous system and lead your state, you stop reacting and you start responding. Calm becomes your signature. Presence becomes your power.

Each of these forces became part of me. Not because I read about them, but because I lived them. And that's what I want for you. Not just to understand the system. But to *become* it.

You are not behind. You are not broken. You are not too late. You are ready. And the tools are in your hands now.

EXERCISE: YOUR SIX INNER FORCES ALIGNMENT MAP

Now let's make it practical. This exercise brings all the six Inner Forces together in one weekly system. Do this simple weekly exercise to give you a clear picture of where you stand and to guide you in a practical way to keep strengthening your Edge.

When one force lags, it drags down the rest. This exercise shows you where to focus, so you can raise your lowest score and keep all six forces strong.

1. Score each force from 1–10
Ask yourself these questions to guide your scoring:

- **Mind Power** – Do I know my "why, what and first step" each day?
- **Confidence LOOP** – Am I acting from "I can/I am" consistently?
- **Inner Flame** – Do I feel energized by what I'm doing this week?
- **Refuse to Lose** – Do I keep promises to myself when it's hard?
- **Performance Edge** – Am I doing the high-payoff work, well and on time?
- **Ice-cool Composure** – Do I stay steady when the stakes spike?

Your scores could be:

- 0–3 = off track
- 4–6 = mixed
- 7–8 = strong and reliable
- 9–10 = elite and world class

2. Identify your lowest score
That is your Focus Force this week. If there's a tie, choose the one draining the most energy or blocking results.

3. Choose one action
Go back to the chapter for your lowest force. Read and reflect on the ideas and exercises there, then decide on one area that resonates and would most improve your score. Write down a few ways you could put it into practice this week, then pick one and schedule it.

4. Review next week
Did your Focus Force rise by +1? If yes, keep going until it's at least 8. Then move to the next lowest.

Your first aim is to bring every force to an 8 – solid and dependable. Only then should you push for 9 or 10, which represent rare levels of sustained excellence. The logic is simple: it's better to be strong across all forces than world class in one while weak in another.

Small, steady gains compound into extraordinary growth – and that's how your Infinite Edge becomes unshakeable

Time: your ally

If there's one final tool that multiplies every force you've built in this book – it's time. Not more of it. Just a better relationship with it. Because time is not a passive resource – it can be your active ally. There are only three ways to use time:

- You can **waste it** – in distraction and delay.
- You can **spend it** – reacting, surviving and ticking boxes.
- Or you can **invest it** – with intention, with presence and purpose.

The elite don't always work longer, but they do work deeper. They know their time is sacred.

One of the most powerful ways to shift your relationship with time is to create a space where clarity can live. Not noise. Not motion. Just quiet. Five minutes of true reflection will outperform five hours of mindless motion, every time:

- Five minutes a day. A chair. A journal. A pen.
- No phone. No pressure. Just you – checking in with who you are becoming.

And when you reflect – track.

- Don't just race forward. Look back.
- Capture lessons. Celebrate wins.

Your past starts working *for* you – reminding you of your strength, showing you the progress you've earned. Over time, belief compounds. You don't just hope you're growing – you *know* you are.

This is how you own your minutes. Because when you lead time, time responds. You shape it – and it shapes you.

This is *your* time

None of us want to reach the end of our lives filled with regrets about the things we didn't do, the words we never said, the freedom we never claimed.

Bronnie Ware, a palliative care nurse, spent years beside people in their final days. She listened closely to their reflections and wrote down what they wished they'd done differently in her book, *The Top Five Regrets of the Dying*. They didn't speak of missed promotions or failed careers. They spoke of life. Of joy. Of truth. Their most common regrets?

- *I wish I'd had the courage to live a life true to myself, not the life others expected of me.*
- *I wish I hadn't worked so hard.*
- *I wish I'd had the courage to express my feelings.*
- *I wish I'd stayed in touch with my friends.*
- *I wish I'd let myself be happier.*

But you're not at the end. You're here. You still have time. You still have choice. That means your story isn't finished – it's still being written. And right now, you get to shape it.

I believe in you

In all my years of coaching, I've never once heard someone say, "I failed because I was encouraged too much." If anything, people wish they'd had more belief poured into them. So let me say it clearly: *I believe in you.* I believe there's more in you. And I believe that if you use your time with purpose, with clarity and with conviction, what you create from here could be extraordinary.

I see it time and again with the clients I work with – people who once doubted themselves, now achieving breakthroughs they never thought possible. Ordinary people stepping into extraordinary lives. And that same potential is in you.

You've already done something remarkable: You have a new awareness of six Inner Forces most people never think about. You've learned how to:

1. Sharpen your mind
2. Loop belief into being
3. Light your Inner Flame
4. Stand firm when quitting was easier
5. Choose to show up
6. Stay composed when the pressure is on.

That's not small work. That's system-level growth.

So, don't wait for more time or the right time. Don't wish away what's in front of you. Use it. Own it. Not with pressure – but with presence. Not with fear – but with faith. This is your time.

Your confidence mantra

This book wasn't just about learning – it was about *becoming*. About shaping a deeper, stronger version of you. Through your quiet inner strength forged by the six Inner Forces you've discovered.

Because confidence is more than a feeling. It's the quiet certainty that keeps showing up – grounded, focused, fully present – even when doubt tries to pull you away. And when you live that way consistently, something powerful happens. Confidence becomes part of you. It becomes how you move, how you decide, how you lead.

So here's your anchor – your mantra. Five simple lines to guide you when things get loud, messy, or uncertain. Repeat it often. Write it down. Speak it out loud. Let it steady you when pressure rises, and lift you when momentum fades. Because when this rhythm becomes part of you, your confidence won't need to shout. It will speak through everything you do:

- Think this is your time – AWARENESS
- Feel this is your time – BELIEVING
- Act like this is your time – DOING
- Persist like this is your time – BECOMING
- Trust this is your time – FAITH

What comes next

Now it's time to look forward. Because self-mastery isn't the destination – it's the beginning. The next chapter of your evolution is about *others*.

You've mastered yourself. Now master the impact you have on the world around you. The world doesn't just need more high performers. It needs high performers who raise others with them. It needs people who lead with integrity. Who coach with compassion. Who live with conviction and lift others through their presence.

That's what's coming. The next evolution. To lead. To love. To leave a legacy. To use your Infinite Edge not just to win – but to build others who win too.

The system is yours. The tools are in your hands. You've built the foundation. Trained the forces. Forged the identity. Now go make the world better – one bold step at a time.

A personal note from James

Thank you for reading this book. My hope is that somewhere in these pages, something clicked. Something stirred. Something reminded you of who you really are – and who you're becoming.

If this book moved you, please: Pass it on. Share it. Talk about it. Review it. And most of all – live it. Every page was written for people like you.

Because the world needs what's in you. And now you've got what you need to give it.

ABOUT THE AUTHOR

"James Vincent has created the personal mastery system every leader needs."

Jamil Qureshi

James Vincent is one of the world's leading voices in coaching – a high-performance expert with over 50,000 hours coaching Olympians, CEOs, leaders and thousands of business coaches worldwide. From elite sport to elite business, James brings the mindset of champions to the masses – helping everyday people win in life, work and leadership.

Blending Eastern philosophy with Western performance psychology, James distils the evergreen principles of human achievement into clear, practical and powerful tools anyone can use.

Want to become a coach? Let's talk

James is not just a strategist or speaker – he's a coach. And this book is your invitation to unleash the coach within.

Since the year 2000, James has had the privilege of coaching thousands of business owners, leaders and elite performers. But what lights him up even more? Coaching coaches. He's helped ordinary people become extraordinary coaches – many who now earn seven figures, lead with purpose and enjoy more freedom than they ever imagined. If you've ever felt called to lead, guide or make a deeper impact in the world, this might be your moment.

Like **Gary Keating** – a successful business owner and UK Entrepreneur of the Year. He was looking for a change, and now he is coaching and helping many other entrepreneurs earn the money and live the life they deserve. James has coached him for over a decade, and during that time Gary rose to become the world number one business coach. Coaching didn't just transform his clients' lives – it transformed his own.

Or **Anu Khanna** – a powerhouse in every sense, former Managing Director at the Ikea Group. Today, she's one of the top two female business coaches in the world. She's built wealth, freedom and a level of impact most only dream of. And it all started with one decision ... to coach. She's a woman of exceptional character, consistency and care, and coaching gave her the vehicle to unleash all of it.

Or **Marcus Ellis** – Olympic medallist in Badminton. James started coaching Marcus when he was a young, ambitious boy from Huddersfield. He went on to become the first Briton to win an Olympic medal in a men's Badminton event. During that era, James also coached three players into the world's top five – and several more into the top ten. These incredible people became walking examples of what belief, coaching and relentless execution can create.

These aren't just success stories – they're real people who said yes to a bigger future.

- So if you're ready to explore what it might look like to become a coach,
- Or you would like to bring James in to speak at your organization, business, school or conference,
- Or to benefit from exclusive tools and coaching insights ...

... connect with James now:

jamesvincentofficial.com

ACKNOWLEDGEMENTS

No one wins alone. And I've never believed that more than I do now.

To my wife, Ceri – you are the quiet strength behind every word of this book. While I've been out building this mission, you've been holding up the world behind the scenes. You've carried the invisible load, made the sacrifices and kept our family strong so I could pour myself into this. That's not background support – that's partnership at the highest level. I love you more than I can put on paper. None of this happens without you.

To our amazing children – Elliot, Emilie and Olivia – you are my greatest source of joy, inspiration and perspective. Every time I write about belief, courage and becoming your best, I think of you. This book may be for the world, but its heartbeat is for you. I hope one day you read it and feel the strength of what's possible – not just out there, but inside you. You've given my life its truest meaning. I'm so proud to be your Dad. This isn't just my journey. It's ours. We've made sacrifices as a family. We've grown together through it. We've built a life full of purpose, laughter and love – and I wouldn't trade it for anything. You are my why. You are my Edge. You are my home.

To my Mum – thank you for being a rock in my life growing up. Your strength, warmth and support created the foundation I've stood on ever since.

To my Dad – thank you for planting belief in me from the beginning. You told me I could do anything, and I've been living that belief ever since.

To Rod Fletcher – my PE teacher when I was nine – thank you for being the spark. You helped ignite something in me that still burns bright today.

To Harry and Barbara Jarvis – thank you for more than just teaching me how to perform. You taught me how to coach. And not just well – but at the highest level.

To my mentors in sport: Patrick Duffy, Mark Bawden, Sir Clive Woodward and Frank Dick OBE – each of you changed my life. You helped me find clarity, strength and strategy when it mattered most. Your wisdom echoes through everything I do.

To Brad Sugars – no one has taught me more. Your mentorship has shaped my thinking, my leadership and my life.

To Ian Christelow and Julie Wagstaff – you are beacons of belief, principles and partnership. Thank you for the trust, autonomy and shared vision. Our teamwork is a force in its own right.

To the ActionCOACH coaches across the world – thank you for allowing me to coach you. I've gained as much as I've given. Every conversation shapes me. Every breakthrough sharpens me.

To my two greatest silent mentors – Napoleon Hill and Dale Carnegie – your work lives through mine. I am, in many ways, a living model of both of you combined.

To the legends I've had the privilege to call friends – Brad Sugars, Marshall Goldsmith, Daniel Priestley, Marcus Sheridan, Uri Geller, Jeffrey Gitomer, Donald Miller, Jamil Quershi, Kevin Sinfield, Jamie Waller, Michael Heppell, Stephen Mulhern – thank you. Every one of you has left a fingerprint on my journey. Your generosity, wisdom and belief have meant more than you know.

And to the countless other people I learn from every single day – clients, peers, teammates and family – you remind me what this work is really about: becoming better, together.

This book carries my voice – but it holds *your* influence.

Thank you, from the bottom of my heart.